T0043812

Touched By God

1767-KING

Touched By God

Testimonies

Virginia King

1767-KING

Copyright © 1996 by Virginia King.

ISBN #:   Softcover   0-7388-3490-4

All rights reserved. No part of this book may be reproduced or transmitted in
any form or by any means, electronic or mechanical, including photocopying,
recording, or by any information storage and retrieval system, without permission
in writing from the copyright owner.

This book was printed in the United States of America.

To order additional copies of this book, contact:
Xlibris Corporation
1-888-7-XLIBRIS
www.Xlibris.com
Orders@Xlibris.com

CONTENTS

DEDICATIONS

I was born to a young couple. I was the youngest of three children. My mother said I was a difficult birth, because I came out feet first. she would often remind me, that it was a miracle she and I lived passed the birth. Because of this she felt I was different, special, set aside for God.

Mamma had one rule that was unchangeable. Everyone in our house went to church, no exceptions. Rain or shine she herded us off to the little Methodist church across the tracks from our house. It was there I fell in love with Jesus. I knew *He* could do anything. I trusted *Him* with my life at a very young age.

I didn't know, at the time, when my mother was sending me to every church service, and to every youth camp, that she was preparing me to be able to live without her. I was eight years old when my mother was killed. I saw her red blood flow on the street near our house. For years to come I couldn't eat or wear anything red without screaming and hiding.

Slowly as time went by the seed my mother had planted inside of me began to grow. I found myself talking to Jesus and God. Soon the pain in my heart began to subside, and memories of my mother were not so painful. I remembered the happy times we spent together. I began to read my Bible. I had an insatiable desire to read the Bible. By the time I was nine years old I had read the Bible from Genesis to Revelations. The Lord had taken away all my pain and replaced the pain with a burning desire to serve *Him*. I dedicate this book to my mother Beatrice King who had enough understanding to know that I needed to learn about the God who made me.

I also dedicate this book to my grandmother, Henrietta Oliver, who continued my mother's tradition of teaching us about the Lord, and sending us to church. I shall never forget the many nights I awoke to hear her praying. She thought everyone was asleep, so she cried out to the Lord for help in time of trouble. Sometimes she would pray all night. I praise God for that praying spirit she passed on to me.

I am also grateful to the many wonderful ministers of the Gospel of Jesus Christ who have taught and led me in the ways of God with their godly example. One of these ministers is Pastor F. A. Sullivan, a godly woman, who taught me more with her example than with her words. However, I must say she was the first minister who after I heard her preach the "Word", I came away saying, "did not our hearts burn within us as *HE* spoke with us by the way." Because Jesus used her so mightly to preach the "Word". Her late husband, Pastor James Sullivan was also a powerful man of faith, who spoke the truth in love. I praise God for their teachings and their godly examples.

The greatest dedication I can make is to the Lord God who gave *His* son Jesus to die for my sins, and made it possible for me to be filled with *His* Holy Spirit. If there be any praise or glory let it go to the *One* who deserves it- The Lord God and Jesus my Lord. Amen.

FORWARD

I have believed the report of the Lord. and the *Arm* of the Lord has been revealed to me. Therefore my life has never been the same again. Once the Lord is allowed to take control of our circumstances He does just that. Our surrendering to the will of the Lord starts us on the adventure of our life. I have seen God do things I never thought possible, until I felt the power of the Holy Ghost. I know that the Lord is real, and when *He* touches a life we are never the same again.

This book was born out of a passion to record some of the great things the Lord does in the life of an ordinary child of God. It contains instances where I was led by, and instructed by the Lord. I saw the rewards of being obedient to a loving God.

I never want to forget the goodness of the Lord. I want to remember all that He has done for me and others. This book is a book of testimonies of the goodness of God. Prayerfully read this book and let the Lord touch you, and rekindle, or start a fire in you that will cause you to say, you too have been touched by God.

LOVE JENNY

LEARN ABOUT JESUS

One of my fondest memories was walking with my aunt to the Southside of town to shop and visit friends. This area of town was a little rough. It was not unusual to see drunk people fighting or staggering down the street. I was not allowed in this part of town unless I was accompanied by an adult.

My aunt, who was a tall slender fair skinned woman, held my hand as we went from store to store. As a six years old child, I was fascinated by the people I saw, especially the drunk people. Watching them stagger, and listening to their slurred speech was funny to me. However, I dare not laugh, for aunt-tee said, this was sad that anyone would be drunk this early in the morning. So to be like my aunt, whom I admired and loved, I thought in my mind, "how sad."

This particular morning aunt-tee stopped to say hi to a lady who we'll call Ms. Sue. She was on the porch when we arrived. She was the oldest woman I had ever seen before.

There was something about Ms. Sue that was different. It was as if she was surrounded by peace and love. She was like a flower blooming in the desert.

She looked at me and said "Do you go to Sunday School little one?" Aunt-tee replied, "yes, she goes every Sunday. She loves church." "If you can say a Bible verse for me I'll give you some candy." She said to me. My eyes lit up, I know a Bible scripture I said.

"For God so loved the world that He gave His only begotten Son that whosoever believeth in Him should not perish, but have everlasting life." John 3:16 Kings James Version

"Oh, that is so good," she said as she handed me a piece of candy. "She knows her Bible" Aunt-tee said. "I tell you what, Ms. Sue said, pointing a wrinkled finger in my direction, if you can tell me a Bible verse every time you come by my house, I will give you a special treat." OK I said, happy to have such a deal. She gently cupped my face in her hands and said, "God will make you strong and wise. Give Him thanks for everything before you eat it and always say a Bible verse. For our food is sanctified by the Word of God and by prayer."

From that day on I prayed, and said a Bible verse before I ate anything. Sometimes I would pray and say a different Bible verse for each individual potato chip or for each piece of food. I studied my Bible so I'd know more verses.

Ms. Sue kept her word. For each new Bible verse I learned she gave me a special treat. The treat was a small toy or one piece of candy, but to me it was my treasure.

The more scriptures I learned, the more I began to talk and fellowship with Jesus and God.

It was then that I noticed that I was never sick. Everyone around me had colds and flus, and they would cough on me, and I'd drink from their cups, but I never seemed to get what they had. My grandma noticed it too. She said, "you are so blessed to have such a strong healthy body. You are never sick."

The disadvantage of being healthy was that I was constantly having to wait upon those who were sick which meant I couldn't go out and play.

When I felt I could take no more of please bring me soup or please bring me crackers, I complained to my grandmother. Why do I have to wait upon everyone? Why can't I be sick, and they wait upon me? I asked. 'God made you strong and healthy, she said, being sick is no fun."

Grandma said being sick was no fun, but I noticed that everyone who was sick got special hugs, kisses, and food. All I got was a pat on the head, and a "good girl" remark. Mama also said God made me strong. So I decided to ask Him to make me sick.

I explained to God that everyone who was sick got special treatment, and I wanted to be treated special too. So could He please let me get sick.

Nothing happened for several months, but when my best friend's birthday party came around, I could not go because I had a cough. I tried to explain to my grandmother that I was well enough to go, but she would not hear of it. I had to stay home all by myself with my grandma who hugged me, kissed me and brought me special foods. I was so miserable. Never again did I ask the Lord to make me sick again. Missing my best friend's party was the worst thing that could happen to this nine years old girl.

Because I studied His Word, God made me smart in school too. I always brought home "A"s on my papers. I was tested when I was in the second grade. They told my grandmother I was able to do six grade work, and they wanted to move me up several grades. Grandma would not agree to this, because she said I was already small for my age. She was afraid the older children would hurt me. So I remained in my regular grade until I was older.

When I became a teenager, I wanted to be like my friends. I didn't want to be different. I remember one day when I ran in from school, and told my grandmother I wanted to get a white blouse for school. "Why do you want to get the blouse", she asked. I want it because my best friend has one and its beautiful. She looked at me and said, "If you had told me you wanted the blouse because you saw it, and you liked it, I'd get it for you. But wanting it because your friend has one is not a good reason to want anything. What if your friend drinks will you drink to be like her? Learn to be your own woman. Don't let anyone else decide what you like and don't like." I was crushed, but I knew she was right. I had to find my likes.

I was taught at a young age that a woman should dress modestly. One day I was talking with a couple of girls I knew, I was visiting at their house. One of the girls said, "there is this one girl I can't stand, because she wears her dresses so long." Really, I asked, who is she? It's you she said, all the boys in the neighborhood think you are special, and it's all because you wear those long dresses. I'm sorry if that offends you I said, but my grandma says a woman should respect herself enough to cover herself. The girl had no reply, so we went on with our game.

I'm glad the church I attended believed in women dressing modestly. I don't believe a woman has to wear a dress to her ankles to be modest, and neither did the church. However, we were taught that when a woman sat down her dress should cover her knees, so that when she relaxed her legs a little, the whole story wouldn't be told, so to speak. In plainer terms people would not be able to see up her dress. I praise God for godly women who dress modestly, and are not ashamed to be different.

TRAGEDY STRIKES

My middle sister was in a gym class at school when she hurt her leg. She was doing one of the classroom activities when she fell. She cried, and the teacher had her sit out the whole class. Her leg continued to hurt, and she continued to cry. The school sent her home.

She didn't call anyone to pick her up. She walked home. By the time she got home she said her leg was fine. It didn't hurt anymore. This girl had always been a tomboy. She climbed trees and fences. If she said she wasn't hurt. She usually wasn't hurt.

But this time was different. Weeks passed and grandma noticed my sister was limping a little. She asked her about the limp. My sister said there was no pain. Grandma and her friend noticed the leg was smaller. They took my sister to the doctor.

After the doctor examined my sister, he asked grandma if she had fallen recently. Grandma told him she said she had fallen at school, but that she had no pain by the time she got home. The doctor explained to grandma that my sister had been bleeding internally since the fall. He said he would have to test the cells for cancer, but things did not look good.

The test results came back positive. My sister was diagnosed with cancer in the marrow of her bone. The next few months were like a living nightmare.

The doctor started my sister on chemotherapy. He said he was hoping the chemotherapy would slow the spread of the cancer cells. My sister got progressively worse. I watched in horror as my beautiful sister of five feet five inches tall and 110 pounds turn into an 80 pounds bag of bones. I watched as she could no longer hold food or water on her stomach.

It seemed her body had become her enemy. Everything the doctors tried failed. She spent her last days screaming in pain because the drugs the doctor gave her no longer helped.

I felt so helpless. I couldn't help her. I just wanted to wake up and realize that everything had just been a bad dream. But it wasn't a dream, it was real.

There are no words that could describe the hurt I felt the night I said goodbye to my sister for the last time in this world. I was her big sister. I was suppose to protect her. I could not help her.

I couldn't sleep at night, and I couldn't eat. I was like a walking dead person. Everyone kept saying God took my sister. I got angry at God. I now know that God did not take my sister, but at the time I believed what the people said. I became angry with God. I wanted my sister back. I didn't want to live without her.

Everyday, I would go to her grave and weep for hours. My grandmother sent me up North to live with my older brother and his wife. She was hoping a new environment would help me to forget about my sister.

In Illinois my friends introduced me to a doctor who prescribed some very strong sleeping pills. I found out later that, on the streets, they called these pills red devils. The first time I took the pills they made me sleep, but the second time I took the pills, I had to increase the dosage to get to sleep. The pills made me feel all giddy inside, and I didn't think about my sister's death so much. I continued taking the pills until I became hooked on them. These pills were downers or depressants. I had to take uppers or speed to wake my system up so I'd feel like going to work and school.

From that time on I was high everyday. I went to work high, and I went to sleep high. It was the only way I felt I could face reality. The truth is, it was the only way I could escape reality.

One day my girlfriend who lived two houses down from my house called me and said there was a fire in the projects. She wanted to know if I wanted to go with her to check on our friends who lived in that area. I said I would ride over with her. Just before she picked me up I took two uppers and two downers at the same time. I got in the car with her and we headed for the projects.

By the time we got to the projects, and parked I was blinking in and out. I felt like I was floating. I can't explain it, but I knew, I was dying. My friend didn't know what was going on. She tried to get me to walk over to watch the fireman put out the fire, but I was too far gone, She said I wouldn't budge. She thought I was asleep.

I don't know how it happened, but the next thing I knew I was above myself looking down on myself sleeping in the car. I was out of my body. I looked at my body and it wasn't breathing. I knew I was dead. Suddenly I was no longer in the car. I was in a tunnel a dark tunnel that appeared to have a small flicker of light far , far ahead. I Was being guided toward the small flicker of light. In my mind I thought its over, I'm dead, thank God, its over. The closer I got to the small flicker of light, the more the flicker looked like a flame of fire. As I got closer to the light, from out of nowhere I heard my grandmother praying. She was crying and screaming out to God to please save me. Her voice was so loud it hurt my ears. I screamed out, please stop it, just let me go. But she wouldn't stop praying. Soon her praying filled the entire tunnel, and it seemed nothing existed but her praying and crying out to God for me.

The next thing I knew I was back in my body, and my friend was driving us home. I looked over at her, and said stop the car. I barely got out before I started regurgitating. I regurgitated for what seemed like forever, before I fell to the ground exhausted. My friend was crying hysterically, she said, "oh my God I thought you were going to die or something. I've never known anyone to throw-up so much for so long." I'm OK I said. She took me home.

I knew God had pumped my stomach and saved my life. But I was still miserable and sad. I decided that day that I wanted to die, but I knew I didn't have the courage to take my own life.

I prayed, and I asked the Lord to take the life He had given me, because I was too miserable to live. I prayed this way for several weeks. Finally one day while I was praying, the Lord spoke to my mind and said, "If you die now where will you spend eternity?" Eventhough, I had seen myself in a dark tunnel I didn't think I would go to Hell. Hell was a place for bad people. I was a good person.

I told God I was a good person. I started seeing in my mind good things I had done, but for every good thing I saw I had done, I also saw a bad thing I had done. I came to the conclusion that if I died I would go to Hell.

I remembered what my Sunday School teachers had taught about Hell. They said it was a place of torment, and darkness, and fire. A place of eternal torment. I thought, my life is already a life of torments, I don't want to go to a worse place of torments.

I prayed again, this time I asked the Lord to please save me first, so that when I died I could go to Heaven. After you save me I said, then I want you to take my life, because I don't feel life is worth living.

That night I had a strange dream. I dreamt I was sleeping in bed and I awoke from sleep, and I was completely changed physically. My hair and skin were completely different. I pondered in my mind what the dream meant, but I had no idea what it meant. I liked the idea of being a completely different person though.

When I went to class that morning I met a friend I had gone to high school with. He stopped me and started talking to me about Jesus. He told me the Lord had placed me on his mind and he had desired to tell me about his new found faith. I was surprised to hear he knew Jesus. In high school he never mentioned anything about Jesus or religion. I told him I knew I had strayed from the Lord, and I wanted to come back to Him. I just needed to know how to come back. He prayed with me and I confessed to the Lord that I was a sinner and I needed the saving grace of His Son Jesus to become real in my life. I told Him I needed Him to save me. I felt God's presence and I knew that He was with me, I also knew that this was just the beginning. I knew there was more God had for me. It was as if I could hear God whisper, there's more, this is just the beginning!

UNIVERSITY STUDENTS GET THE SPIRIT

I was a student at the University of Illinois. I had recently accepted the Lord Jesus as my Lord and Savior. I had been brought up in the Methodist denomination, and I didn't understand what everyone meant by being filled with the Spirit. I didn't know one could receive Him. I saw the Spirit as just the third part of the Trinity. I didn't know He could live inside of a person, especially me.

I was a member of a campus Christian group. We met everyday at lunch time for prayer. It was at one of these meetings one of the brothers announced, a preacher from Chicago was coming to our campus for a meeting, and we would learn more about the Holy Spirit. We were all excited because most of us knew very little about the Holy Spirit.

Later that week, I stopped at a Mcdonald's for lunch. I met an older man there who started talking to me about the Holy Spirit. He told me the Lord wanted to fill me with His Spirit. He was a kind man who patiently entertained my questions about the Holy Spirit. Later, I excused myself and rushed off to class. It was through this man, I began to understand the third person of the Trinity. I never saw the man again.

Some weeks before the preacher from Chicago was to come, we had a bad storm in our area. There was thunder, lightening, and rain that seemed never ending. I lived on campus in a house for girls only. It was a large beautiful old house several girls and I decided to share. That particular weekend all the girls, except one who worked nights and myself, decided to go away for the weekend. I was left alone in the house on the worse night ever. When I got home that night I couldn't get the downstairs light switch to come on. I walked up the stairs to my bedroom in the dark. I felt fear and I tried to think of the Lord, but it was difficult to think of the Lord while I was feeling fear. From out of nowhere I heard a voice speak to my mind and say, "I'll give you power to cast out these same demons that torment you." I knew the Lord was speaking to me, and I knew He meant to comfort me, but in pitch-black darkness the thought of demons being there made me more afraid. I quickly ran up the stairs to my room and locked the door.

To my surprise the light in my room worked just fine. It helped having the light on, but for some reason I still felt a lot of fear. Every frightening movie I had seen came back to mind, every fearful incident I had been involved in, came to mind, everything that made me afraid came to mind. I heard a voice inside my head telling me to run away from the fear. The voice said "run, run and never stop running." I was beginning to think someone was in the house besides me and I thought I should run. Then I heard a voice say "if you run, you must stop running sometime, you can't run forever." I thought to myself, that's right I would have to stop running sometime, so running is not the answer.

In frustration I cried out to God and said, oh Lord, if you are there, please do something. please help me. When I said this a great peace came over me. For the first time since I'd returned home that evening I didn't feel afraid.

Several hours had passed since I'd returned home, I needed to go to the bathroom, and now I wasn't afraid anymore. I got up and I went to the bathroom. I knew everything was fine.

When I returned to my room, the room was all lit-up like the sun had come inside. The room was glowing, I flicked the light switch to see if it was the light glowing, but with the light switch off the room still glowed. I looked out the window and said, maybe Jesus did come. I turned to hang up my housecoat, and as I turned *He* walked right through me. I felt the hem of *His* garment as it touched my leg. *He* said "Jesus loves." When *He* walked inside of me I felt a purity I had never known before.

He stood in front of me and He said. "this is what it means to be completely subject to the will of God." He touched my head. When He touched me I was gone, I no longer existed. Jesus was living in me and only Jesus and His words and His ways came out of me.

The room went back to normal and what I now know was a vision from God was over. I never again doubted the Lord's existence and my fear was gone.

The following week the preacher from Chicago came. He preached a glorious sermon about the Holy Spirit. At the conclusion of the sermon he asked how many people wanted to receive the Holy Spirit baptism. The place was packed with students. Fifty or more students, myself included, went forward to answer the call. They took us to a small room for prayer. In the prayer room the minister told us the Holy Spirit was God's gift to us. He asked us what we usually did when someone gave us a gift. We say thank-you I said. "That's right", he said and we are going to put our minds on Jesus and start thanking *Him* for filling us with the Holy Ghost, because *He* is the one who baptizes us with the Holy Spirit. As soon as I knelt in prayer, I felt the presence of the Lord, it over-whelmed me. I had never felt God's presence so strongly before. I felt out of control and that frightened me. When I drew back the presence of the Lord lifted.

I decided it might be a good idea to sit and watch what happened to the others first before I ventured any futher into this new world where God was in control.

My eyes fell on my best friend, he was a graduate student who was working on his PH.D.. in math. He was praising God and saying thank-you Jesus when all of a sudden his face lit-up, like he had swallowed a light-bulb. He started speaking in another language. He looked so happy. I'd never seen him so happy before.

I looked around the room and all the students were speaking in other languages. I saw a guy, who was from the southside of Chicago, speaking fluent French. Everyone was jumping around laughing and speaking in other languages. Everytime they got ready to say something it came out in another language.

When they all finally settled down, one by one they began to talk about how great they felt, how close to God they felt and how happy they felt. Everyone of the students who had come had received the Holy Spirit, except myself and another student who had fallen asleep ,because he had worked the night before.

As the others talked I began to feel jealousy and anger. I wanted the joy these students had, and I was angry at God for leaving me out. I began to tell Him so in my mind as the others talked. Lord, I said, if I had a gift for you, you wouldn't have to beg me for it, I'd just give it to you. The Lord spoke to me and said, "If you then being evil, know how to do good things, how much more shall your heavenly Father give the Holy Spirit to them that ask Him." I can't explain it but I knew exactly what He meant. It was much later in my walk with the Lord I found the words *He* spoke to me were in the scriptures.

In my mind I agreed with what the Lord had said. I was basically evil, but I did some good things. God on the other hand is pure goodness and never does evil, so He will do more than what we ask or think. I caught on to faith and I began to praise God in my mind. I was saying thank-you Jesus in my mind when in my mind's eye, I saw a large pitcher raised above my head. The pitcher was filled with joy. As it was poured out upon me I felt joy flowing throughout-out my body.

Overwhelmed with joy and the presence of the Lord, I opened my mouth to say thank-you Jesus, and strange words began to flow out. I was speaking in tongues and I too was filled with the Holy Spirit.

The Lord knew exactly what I needed. I had been grieving over a sister who had died three years prior to this event. When the Holy Ghost came in all the grief left. I never cried another tear. I never spent another day grieving at her grave. When thoughts of my sister came they were pleasant thoughts. The Lord had delivered me I could smile again.

BAD WEATHER

We had a bad storm and I was on campus. I wanted to get to a place where I felt safe. It was raining, lightening, and thundering. I just wanted to get away from it all. I remembered running home, and hiding behind buildings whenever the lightening flashed. As I was running and hiding behind the buildings lightening flashed and lit up the area around me. The Lord spoke to me out of the lightening, He said, "Why are you hiding?" I said, because I'm afraid. "Why are you afraid?" He asked. I'm afraid of the lightening and the thunder, I responded. "Who made the thunder and the lightening? He asked. That was the first time I thought about who made the thunder and the lightening. I said. You made it. Yes, I made it, said the Lord, and you are my child. I see you and I love you. I won't hurt you. My fear left me with that revelation. My Father was in control, and He would watch over me for good. I am no longer afraid of the lightening and the thunder. God controls the lightening, and the thunder.

THE DREAM

I had a strange dream one night. I dreamt the other Christian students and I were standing on a street corner and someone in a car drove up and shot all of us in the head. Eventhough, I was shot in the head, I was still alive. I tried to help the others, but they were all dead. I walked away, still bleeding from the head wound, but I was alive. The dream ended. I awoke. I prayed the horrible thing I saw in the dream wouldn't come to pass. The Lord told me the dream's meaning was spiritual and I'd understand by and by.

I worked after school in those days. I told the Lord I had very little time to pray, then I asked His guidance. He took me to the scripture where Jesus said, If a man loses his life for my sake, he will find it. I knew I had to put the Lord first in my life. I prayed and asked the Lord what I should do and where I should go. He told me to leave school and go to Mississippi. Leaving school I could understand, but going to Miss. could not be an option. A friend of mine told me about an older lady who needed help with her ministry in New York city, so I decided to go there.

In New York city I learned what happens to disobedient children. Everything that could go wrong went wrong. The older woman was a backslidden Christian who hated Spirit-filled Christians. She made my life miserable. There were sinners who knew her who told me they were going to kill her or put out a contract on her because she was so mean to them. I'd tell them about the Lord, and they'd listen, because they said, I had to have God to take her abuse and still help her.

The pastor at the Methodist church the older woman forced me to go to, said he had a ministry for smelling out money. He said he knew when someone in the church had a lot of money. I was hungry for the WORD. I wanted God, but now I was farther away from Him, than I was before. The tip of the iceberg came when the city of New York went bankrupt. Everything was so hard for me because the way of a transgressor is hard. I came to New York on my own. I paid a high price for my disobedience. Finally, I cried out to the Lord in submission and repentance, saying I'd do whatever He wanted me to do. The Lord told me to go to Miss. I obeyed.

When I had only been in Miss for a few months, the Lord let me meet pastors who had recently started a Bible school. It was at this Bible school the Lord taught me how to walk in His ways. He also opened His Word to me and called me into the ministry while at this school.

The Lord brought the dream back to my mind some years later. He showed me how, because of some of the materials taught in some of the classes I was taking at the University of Illinois, I had been wounded in the head. Primarily the wound represented the things I was being taught that spoke against God and things that shook my faith in God. Also my being too busy to put the Lord first in my life didn't help things. Jesus says to us, take my yoke upon you and learn of me. I later finished my degree after I learned God's ways. That's a testimony I'll share later. Just remember the Lord must be first in our life.

I'M HEALED

When I came to the Lord I was sick. I didn't know how sick I was until I went to the doctor. I had started bleeding abnormally and I was having some other physical problems. The first doctor I went to wanted to do what he called a probe operation. This operation, he said would give them an idea of where the bleeding was flowing from. He also said the operation would probably benefit science more than it would benefit me. I decided against the operation. I heard testimonies in the church of the Lord healing people. I made up my mind I would believe God for my healing.

Months passed when I was in Miss.. My condition got worse. I went to another doctor because my grandmother insisted. This doctor examined me and did some lab work. She told me she felt my cells might be cancerous, but she wouldn't know for sure until the lab results came back. When the test results came back she told me my cells were cancerous. The ministers at my church prayed for me, and I began the fight of my life. One minister told me to thank the Lord I was healed every time I felt pain or discomfort. I did just that and everytime I did it the pain got worse. I knew the enemy of our soul was trying to shake my faith. I continued to thank the Lord for healing me.

My family urged me to do whatever the doctors said. The only problem was the doctors weren't giving much hope with anything they recommended. I lost so much blood until my brain cells began to die. I would awake from sleep and not be able to remember where I was or who I was.

The doctor scheduled me to receive blood. I agreed. When I went in the nurse who checked my vital signs said she didn't understand why I was still conscious. According to her my blood level was too low for me to function. I was about to let her stick the needle in my arm and begin the process when I heard the Holy Ghost say don't take this blood. I pulled my arm away and I told her I had changed my mind I didn't want this blood. You know you are putting your life in danger, she said. I know, I said. I went home.

It was about a year later we heard the blood at the clinic, I was to get blood from, was contaminated with the aids virus. The Lord knew this, that's why He told me not to take the blood.

My condition got worse and I got weaker. To complicate matters even more I caught the mumps on one side. I only had it on one side as a child. The doctor said it alone was enough to kill me, since I was so weak physically. I continued to stand on the WORD. I was healed by the stripes of Jesus.

Months later I awoke early one morning, my sheets were drenched in blood as if I had an operation. I heard Jesus saying to me, go into all the world and preach this gospel. I said how can I go anywhere like this, physically I'm sick. He said to me rise and be healed. I tried to get up, but when I moved the bleeding increased. Two more times He said the same words. I knew if I didn't get up now I would never get up. By faith I got up. As soon as my feet touched the floor the bleeding stopped, and I could feel in my body I was healed. What was wrong was now right praise God. I was examined by three or more doctors and they all said the same thing—it was as if you were never sick. We don't have to be sick, the Lord is a healer. He made this body, he can certainly heal it, Amen.

NEIGHBORHOOD WITNESSING

From the first day I got saved I knew I was to tell people about Jesus, and I did. I witnessed to everyone in my neighborhood, sometimes more than once. If they were too busy to talk to me I'd baby-sit or clean house or help in anyway I could, so I could share Jesus with them. Because I was young, and most of these people had seen me grow up, some didn't always take me serious. Some would pat me on the head and say that's so nice you are living for Jesus. After witnessing I would go home and pray for the people I talked with. In spite of everything some of the people said Yes to the Lord.

MRS. R

The Lord began to send me to different ones in the neighborhood. One of these persons was Mrs. R. She was one of the nicest ladies one would ever meet. As I sat talking with her I told her what the Lord had done for me. She began to cry. She told me she had gone to see the doctor earlier that morning; he told her she had cancer and she only had a few weeks to live, maybe a month. I told her the Lord says who lives or dies not the doctor. I said let's pray and ask God what He says. We prayed, the Lord spoke to me and said tell her she has five years. I told her and she received it. I told her the Lord wanted her to turn her life over to Him. She said she wanted to do that, but not just yet. What about your grandmother she said, she thinks you're a fanatic. I told her when she stood before God she wouldn't stand with my grandmother, she'd stand alone, therefore her decision to go all the way with God should be based on God's truth not my grandmother's opinion. Nonetheless she said she'd think about it.

The Lord was true to His Word. Mrs. R. lived for five more years without any complaints from the cancer. At the end of five years the Lord told me to tell her she needed to say yes to His will and live for Him, for her time had come to make a decision. I went to Mrs. R and I told her all the Lord had given me to say. I also told her how much the Lord loved and cared for her. She agreed with everything I said, but when it came to making a decision she said she wasn't ready, she was a member of a little Baptist church and was concerned about what her friends would say if she received the Holy Ghost. Nothing I could say persuaded her. I left her house very sad that day.

About two weeks later when I returned home my grandmother asked me if I had heard about Mrs. R.. I said no, what happened. She said her granddaughter found her dead this morning.

My heart was broken. I went to my room and I cried out to the Lord saying raise her from the dead, I know if she just had another chance she'd say yes. I asked the Lord to let me go lay hands on her and raise her up.

The Lord caused me to fall asleep, as I slept I dreamed. In the dream I was at the train station waiting for Mrs. R.. When the train arrived I rushed up to Mrs. R. saying how happy I was to see her. She did not acknowledge my greeting. She looked right past me and kept walking. I continued to walk behind trying to catch up with her and talk to her, saying how happy I was to see her, but she just kept walking. When she finally stopped it was at my house. I tried to tell her she had another chance. Her face was stern and her answer was no. Then she dropped dead. As I was waking up I heard a voice say even if she was raised from the dead she would not say yes. That was a hard truth for me to receive about someone I loved so much.

THE BOYS

There was a group of boys who would stand if front of the neighborhood store and harass the girls who went by. One day I went that way going to the store for my grandma, and as always I took my Bible along. When I saw the group of boys I felt led to tell them about Jesus and His great love for them. I told them what Jesus had done for me. As I talked I saw some of the boys wiping back tears. I invited them to church. After that I never saw those boys hanging around that store again.

The store owner told me later he had been trying for years, with no success, to get those boys to stop hanging around his store. He went on to say after I talked to them about Jesus, now, everytime they see me coming they scatter.

Another friend told me the boys saw me coming toward the store one day and they said, uh oh, here comes Jenny and you know she's going to start telling us about Jesus, so we'd better go. Years later when I returned home I found most of those boys in church. All God told us to do was to tell them. He does the rest.

AUNT J.

Another one of my favorite people was a lady everyone called aunt J. She was a sweet, fun loving older woman who went to the Methodist church I was brought up in. The Lord sent me to her one evening. I told her how the Lord had healed my body and how good God had been to me. I told her how the Lord wanted to save her and fill her with his Spirit. She told me she knew the Lord, but she wasn't like me. I went on to tell her God wanted us to be like Jesus, and Jesus was a man filled with the Holy Ghost. She agreed, and she looked at me and said, I'm just not ready to go all the way yet. I told her she might not have anymore time to get ready. I told her the Lord had sent me to tell her she had to make a decision now. She told me she was not ready. I felt aunt J's decision was based on the relationship she had with the married man she had dated secretly for years. She knew to go all the way with the Lord meant she had to give him up, and she wasn't ready to do that.

About two weeks later aunt J. had a heart attack in her bathtub and died. A week passed before she was found by her lover. Jesus said, Today is the day of salvation. We need to say Yes to the Lord when He calls.

A TWELVE YEAR OLD GIRL

I was walking down the street one day and I saw a young girl who was about twelve years old. The Lord spoke to me and said tell her she needs to come to me. I approached the girl and I told her about the Lord, and I invited her to come to church. She agreed and I arranged to pick her up.

When I went to pick her up there was no answer at her door, although I'd seen someone peering through the window. I saw her again the next week, the Lord said tell her, I did, and I invited her to come to church. Once again she agreed, but when I went to pick her up, there was no answer at the door.

I saw her again the following week; the Lord said tell her she needs to come to me; the girl saw me and turned and went the other way. I called out to her; she pretended not to hear.

I knew she was from a rough family. Her mother was an alcoholic and she had grown up very fast. she needed the Lord. I saw her again and I cornered her, telling her how much the Lord loved her, and how He could change her life. She listened and said she'd think about what I'd said. I never saw her again.

Sometime after that meeting with her, she was riding in a car with some boys from school. They had decided to visit a nearby town. On the way there the driver ran into another car. Everyone survived except this girl; they said she died instantly of a broken neck; attendants said when they pulled her from the car, eventhough she was dead, her last words rolled out, "am I gonna die, am I really going to die?" Regardless of age we all need to say yes to Jesus as soon as we can.

AUNT CLARA

People knew I lived for Jesus and they knew the Lord used me.
They also knew my aunt was one of the biggest sellers of liquor.
My aunt was sweeter than pie. She'd do anything to help me, but
no matter how much I talked to her about the Lord, and her getting right with God she always had a good answer. Jenny, she'd
say, the Lord knows I've got to take care of myself.

She had more money than anyone in the family. She was near
seventy, living with a man she wasn't married to, because she said,
if she married the government would cut-off her social security
check, and then she could not live comfortable. She did come to
church with me a couple of times and she would pray. The Lord
led me to just pray for her and leave her alone. I did.

Months later my grandma called me and told me they had rushed
my aunt to the hospital. I got to the hospital as quickly as I could.
When my aunt looked up and saw me. She smiled. I could tell she
was relieved I was there. She was giving instructions to her live-in
mate about how to run her business until she got back. I said aunt-tee
you should be praying and seeking the Lord and repenting, not giving instructions about business. She said I will, but I want him to
know what to do. I said aunt-tee you don't know what tomorrow
holds, you may not have this opportunity to pray again. She took my
hand and she said I'm OK now, you're here. I told her she needed to
pray. She smiled and they wheeled her away.

That was the last time I saw her conscious. I stayed in the
hospital room with her. She was in a coma. I began to fast and
pray. I told the Lord I wanted her saved. Everyday and all throughout-out the day, I'd whisper into her ears, aunt-tee call on Jesus,
He loves you and He will save you.

One night, after prayer, when I had fallen asleep, I was awakened and I saw Jesus come into the room. He stood at aunt-tee's bed. I didn't hear anything He said. After He finished what He came to do for her, He turned to me; He never left her bedside; He said, to me "receive strength"; I felt great strength surge through my body; I couldn't move; He walked out the room.

I went to sleep and slept soundly. That night I dreamt I went to aunt-tee's house and the beautiful scarves she liked to put on her tables were laid out. The scarves were whiter than white and they were beautiful. That's all it was to the dream. Aunt-tee died that morning. My prayer is that those white scarves represent her getting things right with the Lord. When I get to the other side I'll know for sure Amen.

A CAR

I was so tired of sharing the family car with my older brother who felt it was his car. Whenever I needed the car he needed it. His need was always greater and more urgent than my need, in his opinion. The only solution was for me to get my own car. I had just started a new job. Maybe, I could afford a new car.

When I got my first check I was so disappointed by the amount of it, I gave the entire amount to the Lord saying, I believe you can do more with this than I can. I didn't know how true a statement that was.

I put in a request for a new car in the prayer circle at church. I told the Lord I wanted a car, and I asked for his guidance.

I was passing by a car lot a few days later, when one car got my attention. I went over to look at it. It was exactly the car I wanted. A salesman came out to greet me. "You can drive off in this car today", he said. I really like this car, its exactly what I want. I said. Well, let's talk, he said. Now how much money do you want to put down on the car. He asked. I don't have any money to put down, I said. In fact I don't have any money. I just started working this week. I tell you what, he said, Give yourself a little time to save up a down payment, and then come back and get a car. I smiled and left to meet my friends.

I met with my pastors later, they were a husband and wife team. I was feeling a little depressed about getting a car, and wouldn't you know it the wife started asking me questions about getting a car. Have you got your car yet? She asked. No, I haven't I said. What are you waiting on. You're a faithful giver, and the Lord honors faithfulness. He won't let you outdo Him. Tell the Lord what you want, and believe Him to do what you desire. Her words really ministered to me. It Was as if God himself was speaking to me. I knew the Lord would help me. I prayed in my mind, Lord, I want that car, please tell me what to do, and please guide me in the way I should go. I believe you I just don't know how or what to do.

The next day I felt led to go back to the car dealership. This time I put my hands on the car and in my mind, I said, I claim this car in Jesus name. This is my car in Jesus name. The dealer walked up and said, You're going to buy that car today? God said its my car, I said, so I know He is going to make a way for me to get this car. God said this is your car. Are you sure God said it? He asked. Yes God said it, I said, and I believe Him. God said it, the man said as if thinking about the statement.

The dealer looked at me and said, I know my company will probably reject your application, but you said God said it, so let's do the paperwork and see what happens.

I went inside and we completed the paperwork. When we finished the paperwork, the dealer said, do you have any money on you, you have to put something down. I searched in my pockets and found a penny. Here I said I'll put this penny as down payment. He took the penny and said, now I know the people in the front office are going to think I'm crazy, and they are not going to approve this application. I thanked the dealer. I left thanking God in my heart for my new car. That was Monday.

Saturday of that week I was having breakfast when my grandmother called to me, and said a man in a green car was asking for me. I went to the door and looked out. There was the dealer in my car. He said, do you still want this car? Yes, I do I said. Then let's go finalize this thing. I rode with the dealer to his office and completed the papers to get my car. The company decided to take a chance with me, because the Lord touched their hearts, and gave me favor. I drove home in my new car. Praise God!

THERE IS POWER IN JESUS NAME!

One of the main or primary functions of my car was picking up people for church. I shall never forget the day I picked up some elementary aged children for summer Bible classes. when I was returning the children to their homes God gave us a miracle. I was waiting to make a left hand turn. I looked in my rear view mirror, and I saw a van coming straight for my car at a high speed. I couldn't turn because there was too much traffic. I couldn't do anything. So I called on the One I know who hears and answers prayer. I screamed Jesus as loud as I could. The van hit my car. It was as if we were cushioned. We did not smash into the other cars as we should have. My car stood still. The thought of being hit by a car frightened one little girl so much, she jumped out of the car and ran to her house which was just down the street.

I checked the children for damage and there was none. The children said they did not feel it when the van hit us. They said they felt a soft cushion against their face as they came forward. That was all they felt.

The policemen came. We found out the man driving the van worked for a flower company. He hit four other cars beside mine. He was on drugs and didn't realize he was going eighty miles an hour. An ambulance arrived and took several people to the hospital. The children and I were the only ones who didn't go to the hospital. Jesus had delivered us.

The mother of the little girl who ran home, came to the scene of the accident with her child. She said I didn't believe my child when she told me that a van had hit your car, and she was in the car when the van hit it. She wasn't hurt or anything. I had to come and see for myself. There is power in the name of Jesus, and there is nothing He will not do to help His people.

By the way there was no damage to my car either. Praise God!

I had another opportunity to see the power in "Jesus" name in action in a mighty way. I was at a Laundromat. I needed to dry some large pieces of fabric. Two girls about eight years old came in, and they proceeded to put their clothes into the washer. Shortly thereafter a young guy about twenty or twenty-one came in. He didn't notice the little girls at all. He put his clothes in a dryer and left. The little girls seemed mesmerized by him though. I heard one of them say," oh he's so cute." The guy got in his car and drove across the street to a gasoline station. The little girls followed the guy across the street. One of the girls was able to get across the street with very little trouble, she watched the flowing traffic, but the other little girl was watching the guy in the car, who was driving away at this time.

I saw the gray van approaching, but I didn't have time to run out to the street, and warn the mesmerized little girl. I screamed Jesus please save her. The van hit the little girl. I ran outside. I saw the little girl land what looked liked twenty or thirty feet from where the van was. Then I saw her jump up and run home.

The people in the van were so upset, they were an older couple on vacation, they were crying, saying, "it was an accident, we didn't mean to hit her, oh please God forgive us." I told them the little girl was all right, but they didn't believe me. "We saw her little body flying through the air, they said, there is no way she could have survived that.

By now the little girl had returned with her grandmother. What happened up here asked the grandmother? She said she got hit by a van, but I told her that was impossible since she was still standing.

I told them I called on Jesus and He saved the little girl. The couple was hugging and kissing the little girl. Thanking God she was all right. The grandmother who was a Christian said she knew only God could have saved her. The little girl was so shakened up she just cried. When we have done all we can do, Jesus, the name above all names will do the rest.

JOE

I was in class when I received a message to call home as soon as possible. I asked another teacher to watch my class while I went to make a call. My brother answered the phone. I could tell he was upset. Please come home I can't tell you over the phone. Is someone hurt I asked? Please just come home. I explained to the principal that I needed to go home as soon as possible. He got someone to substitute for me and I went home.

When I got home everyone was crying or had been crying. They told me that Joe had killed himself. He shot himself in the head.

I was stunned.

My youngest brother was walking around saying over and over to everyone, "he called me, if I had just come over when he called me maybe he wouldn't be dead.

I went in my room to pray for strength. As I prayed I thought of how successful Joe was. He was my grandmother's adopted son. She got him when he was a baby. My mother was an only child until my grandma's cousin gave her Joe. Joe Was a guy who always laughed. He never seemed to be sad. He was tall dark and handsome, and had several lady friends. He was financially prosperous, and he enjoyed bragging about the new car he got every year.

Things seemed to be going well for Joe, until he went to Vietnam. When he returned from the war, the family says he was never the same. I couldn't tell what was going on with him because he always joked about everything. I had prayed for him though, and I had talked to him about giving his life to the Lord. He had let me know that he didn't have time for that, and that he felt God was not real because there was so much suffering in the world.

Several times I tried to talk to him about Jesus, but he would not listen to me.

Now as I sat alone in the room praying, the enemy tried to mock me, "you reached so many others, why couldn't you reach him", I felt that I had lost a battle. As despair tried to settle in, the Lord said to me "people need the Lord", When he said this to me I could see that money, cars, and women was not enough to satisfy a man. People needed the Lord to be totally fulfilled.

I felt encouraged and strengthen in the Lord. I prayed for my family and I asked the Lord to use this situation to save many souls, and to glorify the name of Jesus, so satan would not think he had won a victory.

The Lord answered that prayer. At Joe's funeral the place was packed with his unsaved friends. The Lord used me to minister the "Word of God" to them. When I finished, the altar was filled with his unsaved friends who wanted to know Jesus. God took something bad, and brought something good out of it. Praise His Name!

GRANDMA

In any neighborhood the hardest people to reach are your family. When I first came home and told my two brothers and one sister what the Lord had done for me, they all surrendered their lives to the Lord. My biggest test however, came from my grandmother, who was the leader of our family. She did not think it took, "all that", as she said, to be saved. She said people can overdo anything, and my reading my Bible everyday was overdoing things. It was going to drive me crazy according to her.

My grandmother was one of the sweetest women anybody wanted to meet. She believed in helping all of her neighbors. I shall never forget the time she cooked food for a lady, whom I'll call Ms. Kay. She told me I was to take the food to Ms. Kay and help her in any way she needed help. I didn't want to go to Ms. Kay's house, because she was old and mean. Grandma ignored my desires, and said, no matter how much she finds fault or complains, you are to say yes mam, and be kind and polite. If you are any other way, you'll have to answer to me.

I took the food to Ms. Kay's house. I did exactly what my grandmother said. I was kind and polite. Ms. Kay was her usual mean self. She had returned home from the hospital. Her leg had been amputated, and she had diabetes. She complained about everything I did. I didn't help her up right, I took too long emptying the bed pan. I was not a good helper. I'll try to do better I said. I left as soon as I could, hoping this would be my last time coming to Ms. Kay's house.

Everyday for the next year or so I had to attend to Ms. Kay. I learned to drown out her complaints and just help her. I learned to love her, and understand that she was hurting, and that was why she complained so much. Through this experience I learned how to love in the midst of adversity.

Ms. Kay noticed that I didn't talk back or rebuke her for anything she said to me. She began to soften a little. She still complained but not as much. One day to my surprise, she called me to her wheelchair and she said, thank you for being so kind to me. Your grandmother has trained you well. Grandmother continued cooking food for Ms. Kay, and she continued sending me to help Ms. Kay until the day she died.

I remember another time when I overheard two ladies talking about my grandmother. One lady said, "She thinks she is so pretty because her hair is so long and beautiful. Just wait until she comes to have me style it for her, I'm going to cut it all off."

I tried to tell my grandmother what the ladies said, but she dismissed it as foolishness, and something a child should not be concerned about. She continued to be friends with the ladies. She even let the lady do her hair, and true to her word the lady cut grandma's hair very short.

When I asked grandma about her short hair, she said it was hot and the beautician went crazy cutting. I felt despisement for the beautician, knowing she intentionally cut grandma's hair extra short without her permission.

Whenever, I went by this lady's house I would turn my head away and purposely not speak to her. I did this for two days. The lady came to my grandma's house and told her what I had done.

When I got home from school grandma confronted me. She wanted to know why I was being so disrespectful. I told her I didn't like the lady because she was talking about her. I thought grandma would understand.

My grandmother spanked me. She explained to me that I was to show respect to all grownups regardless. She said, Jesus said love your enemy. Do you think you were showing love by not speaking to that lady, she asked? I don't care what she said about me, God told us to love, and you're going to love, even if it kills you. God, not you, will judge that lady.

She told me to dry my eyes, and go apologize to the lady. I went and apologized to the lady. From that day on, I spoke to everyone two, three, or more times in a day. I remember the neighbors telling my grandmother about me saying, she speaks all the time, she is so friendly. By the way Grandma's hair grew back even longer and more beautiful. The Bible says foolishness is bound in the heart of a child, but the rod of correction will drive it far from the child.

I was older now and I understood what Jesus meant about loving and not hating a little better than when I was eleven. I had been filled with the Spirit and I wanted my grandma to be filled with the Spirit too. I invited grandma to visit my church, but she refused, saying she'd go to her Baptist church where people didn't overdo Christianity. I continued to pray for her.

As time went by she told me, I had really changed. She said, I know the Lord has touched your life. I was glad she could see Jesus in me, but I wanted her to know the joy of being filled with His Spirit.

When she was in her late sixties she had a stroke. I rushed to the hospital to be by her side. When I got there she took my hand and she said, "If the Lord raises me up from here, I'm going to go to church with you." I was so happy to hear that. The Lord did raise her up and she was back home with us the next week.

When Sunday rolled around I asked her about church. She said, "it's too hot today". I asked her the next Sunday and she said, "it's too cold today". I asked her again and she said, "I don't have any nice shoes to wear". I bought her another pair of nice shoes. I asked her again and she said, "my hair isn't acting right today". Considering she had straight hair which she only wore one way, this was a poor excuse. I told her when she decided to go to church with me, she could let me know. I continued to pray for her.

Sometime later, I don't remember how much later, grandma had another stroke. This stroke left her speechless. She'd try to talk and nonsense words would come out. Finally realizing no one understood her words she succumbed to silence. Years passed and her voice was silent.

I was doing some mission work in Japan when the Lord spoke to me, and said, if you want to spend time with your grandma before she leaves you need to go now. I had asked Him to allow me to spend time with her before she died, and He was honoring my request. I returned to America.

I brought grandma to my house. Everyday, I talked about Jesus to her, I played sermons for her, I played gospel tapes for her, and I read the Bible to her. She seemed annoyed at all of this after a while. I worried that she would be lost.

I taught at a nearby school. When I was driving home from work, one day, I was praying the Lord would touch my grandma. The Lord spoke to me and said, when are you going to start believing me for her salvation. I thought I was believing you, I retorted. You fret, you pray, you worry, now it's time to start believing. Start thanking me for her deliverance, He said. I started thanking Him, and from that day on, I just thanked Him for grandma's salvation.

Weeks later the in home nurse noticed the signs of another stroke, so we rushed grandma to the hospital. I stayed at the hospital with her. I was sitting in her room reading when I heard her say, "help him, please somebody help him, please help him. I looked up expecting to see someone at the door. The door was shut and no one was there. I said you're talking, you're talking again. My words fell on deaf ears. It was as if she could not see me. She was seeing something different now.

She continued to pled for someone to help him. Then she said, oh Joe, how did you end up here. She cried and pleaded for someone to help.

I didn't know what to do; I was surprised the nurses, who were in and out, hadn't come in; I prayed and the Lord told me to pray, be quiet and listen. She said, I'll help you Joe, I'll help you. In the bed she moved from side to side and seemed to be hindered on both side from helping. Joe was her adopted son who committed suicide. Finally, in great grief she cried I'm sorry Joe I can't help you, I can't help you. She cried as if her heart was broken.

Suddenly, she stopped crying and started screaming no, no, put me down, I'm not going down there. I laid hands on her and I rebuked the devil and asked the Lord to help her call on Jesus. She started calling on Jesus from the depths of her soul. She screamed Jesus Jesus, please save me, please help me.

I know Jesus appeared to her, because she stopped screaming and said, Jesus, I want to come up there to be with you, I don't want to go down there. I didn't see or hear anything other than the hospital setting and my grandma. Jesus said something to her; I know this because she nodded her head and said yes, yes Lord, I'll do it. She looked up at me. I said, are you all right? She opened her mouth to speak and she started speaking in tongues. She had so much joy. She was laughing and speaking in tongues.

After that experience she couldn't get enough of Jesus. All one had to do to get her attention was start talking about Jesus or praying or reading the Bible. She was so precious. She was also able to speak after this experience. She lived for a year or so.

Then one day she stopped eating, her body temperature dropped; I took her to the emergency room; while waiting with her, in the emergency room, I saw the angel of the Lord come and stand at the head of her bed; he leaned over her; his upper body covered her from head to waist; I waited with her; she held my hand one last time, then she let go; her eyes said goodbye, I'll see you on the other side; she closed her eyes and went to sleep. To be absent from the body is to be present with the Lord, and so shall we ever be with the Lord. Amen.

IN SCHOOL AGAIN

When I finished at the Bible school I returned to college to get my degree. That in itself was a miracle. I had no money for school, but I believed the Lord would make a way. I started off part-time. In a speech class I was taking the teacher said I see in you great potential and he suggested I go and talk to the debate coach. I didn't feel I had time for a debate team, so I thanked the teacher and went my way. When this teacher saw me again he encouraged me to at least go by and talk with the debate coach, you're a natural he said, and they have scholarship money.

Scholarship money was the magic word for me. If I was going to continue my education I needed money. I went by to see the debate coach. She gave me an assignment. I wasn't sure where to start, so I prayed. I was sitting on a city bus watching some teenagers act-up when the Lord showed me how to complete my assignment. I did the work and presented it before the coach. She was very pleased with my work. From that day on I was an official member of the speech/debate team.

We competed in colleges all over the USA. In my first official tournament I took second place; after that I took first in every tournament praise God. I brought home so many trophies until the coach had to find a bigger trophy case.

One of my team mates said to me one time, during our travel, you always win, but its as if you don't win, because all you say when you win is "thank the Lord", why? "It's because I know who deserves the glory I said. I know if it wasn't for the Lord I would not win." "But it's not the Lord who does the work, you go to the library, you study, sometimes all night, so why can't you take some credit for your success." "If I hadn't been taught the right way, I would take the credit and the glory to myself; but I've been taught and I know what's right; The Bible says all the glory and all the honor belongs to God; this is His air we are breathing and without Him we could do nothing." I think he finally got the point, he nodded his head in agreement.

I became popular at tournaments; I began to get offers from other colleges. All of them offered full academic scholarships and other benefits. This is what my coach and I had hoped would happen because the funds at our small school was not enough for a full scholarship. My coach encouraged me to take the best offer.

I prayed and the Lord led me to go with a coach who said, "you are not leaving me until you graduate".

This scholarship gave enough money to pay off the student loan I'd made when I first went to college; it paid for tuition, dorm, and books, with a little left to live on. I was so blessed. I continued with this coach until I graduated with my bachelors.

HE'LL BE HELP IN THE TIME OF NEED

I would pick up people to take them to church during the week. I wasn't working at the time. I hadn't been out of high school that long. Most of the people I picked up couldn't afford to give me gas money, and I didn't feel good about asking them for gas money eventhough I traveled several miles to get them back and forth. I was more than happy to help them. My only problem was I had very limited funds to work with. The church was small and I didn't want to burden them, so I did the best I could. I got a job to help with finance back and forth so I could get people to church.

One day when I was on empty, and trying very hard to get to my job to pick-up my check I ran out of gas. I was stranded on the highway. I prayed for the Lord to send help. It seemed that there were no cars on the highway that day, and the one car I had seen went past me. Part of me wanted to panic and the other part said wait. I heard the Lord speak to my spirit and say that help is on the way. I waited and praised the Lord in song as I waited.

Soon a semi-truck came by and stopped. I told him I had run out of gas. He said no problem, I'll give you some of my gas. I said but isn't your fuel different from mine? He said no, this fuel will do fine in your car. He took one gallon of fuel from his truck and put it in my gas tank. My car started fine. I thanked the man. He left, and I drove to my job and picked up my check and filled up my gas tank.

Later when I was telling someone about the trucker, I remembered that his truck had no logo on it like most semi-trucks have. I didn't think about it when the man was helping me. Maybe he was an angel, maybe he was just a nice man. I think the Lord will just send help when we need it. Whether that help comes from heaven or earth it comes, and that's what's important. He will be help in the time of need.

1767-KING

TONSIL TROUBLE

I had one desire that year, and that desire was to graduate with my BS degree in Speech Pathology. It seemed to me that every evil force had the desire to stop me at all cost. I had a slight cough so I went to the infirmary to get some medicine to hopefully stop the virus. I was given medication that I was allergic too. At home, I had a violent reaction to the medication when I took it. My roommate noticed I was unable to respond and she helped me to the infirmary. I still had the prescription in my purse. When they saw the prescription the doctor knew what caused me to get sick. They treated me and took me off the medication I had been given. I was out of classes for a week recovering. A week I really could not afford considering I had traveled every weekend on the debate team, so I was already behind in my studies. The doctor wrote an excuse, but that didn't stop the depression of falling farther behind from plaguing my every thought. I tried studying during the times I wasn't regurgitating or too discomfited from pain. The enemy of our souls kept a constant vigil. "You're going to fail, you're not going to make it", he said. There were times when I felt so bad I was ready to agree with him. But a small voice deep inside of me said, "what does God have to say about the situation"? I prayed, Lord please help me. Tell me what you have to say.

I felt a calm and a peace I thought had left me. Later, I felt strength to start confessing the Word of God. Everytime I felt sick, I would say "By His stripes I am healed." Any scriptures on healing I could remember I would hold on too for my deliverance. I felt so bad physically until reading was an arduous chore. That is what made the Holy Ghost so precious. He continued to bring back to mind scriptures I had studied or sermons I had heard. He made the Word of God come alive to me.

Gradually, I began to get better, and before the end of the week, I was back in class, having only missed two days of work.

I tried to be careful, but long nights, too much work, and a poor diet made it easier for me to get sick again. It started with a sore throat. Before I knew how it had happened, my tonsils had swollen to the size of small tomatoes. They were so big they made my neck look funny. I didn't want to have them taken out. I didn't want an operation. I didn't want to miss class for a week. So I called on the One I knew could do anything. I called on the Lord. I believed He would heal me.

I stood on the Word of God. I confessed that I was healed by the stripes of Jesus; I confessed that He sent His Word and healed me. I confessed healing is the children's bread. The more I confessed the Word the bigger my tonsils got. It wasn't long before it was extremely painful for me to swallow water, and eating was impossible. I could bearly talk. When I did speak it was very painful.

I knew I had to make a decision. Would I believe the Word of God, that proclaimed I was healed by His stripes; or would I believe my circumstances that proclaimed that my tonsils were swollen, I was in tremendous pain and I was sick. The choice was mine. I chose to believe God, and I had to wait on the Lord to heal me.

While waiting on my healing I tried to do everything I would normally do. This included getting up at five in the mornings to meet with other Christians for prayer. By now, my tonsils were so swollen I could not talk. This particular morning it was a struggle to get going. My mind wanted to go, but my body was not moving. Finally, I struggled out of bed, got ready, and waited in the vestibule to be picked up by my friends.

The vestibule was not heated and the temperature outside was 15 or 20 degrees below 0. It was cold and I felt miserable. As I waited The Holy Ghost started singing a little song in my mind,

"By His stripes you are healed hallelujah, in God's Word it's revealed hallelujah; on the cross of Calvary He did it all just for you and now you're set free hallelujah."

Over and over He sang this song to me and it comforted my spirit. Soon my friends came and we went to church.

At church, I knelt to pray. The Lord told me to open my mouth wide and He would fill it. He told me to praise Him. Opening my mouth was painful, nonetheless I began to praise the Lord and give Him thanks. By faith I just opened my mouth, eventhough most of my talking was going on in my head. The Lord told me to open my mouth again; I did. I just waited before Him, painfully opening my mouth to praise Him for His goodness, as I waited, I began to pray for others.

While praying and praising the Lord, suddenly there was a pop. It sounded like a balloon bursting. The brother kneeling next to me jumped. I smiled as I felt my neck. I knew the Lord had healed me. I examined my neck and my tonsils were back to their normal size; I swallowed and there was no pain. I was truly healed by the stripes of Jesus. I walked out of that prayer meeting totally healed by the power of God.

THE HOLY GHOST

I stopped at a friend's house on my way home from an out of town trip. I had driven all night so I was tired. We'll call this friend S. She was a Navajo girl. When I walked in the door she said, I'm so glad you're back, You have to help me. I will if I can, I said. She went on to say, "everyone at the church has the Holy Ghost, but me; When I ask them how to get the Holy Ghost no one tells me what I should do, they just tell me how wonderful it is to have the Holy Spirit in your life; I must get the Holy Ghost today."

I was so tired I couldn't see straight, but I knew I was not going to be able to say no to her. So I prayed for strength. I don't know where the strength came from, but I felt revived.

We went into her bedroom to pray without interruptions, and so we wouldn't wake the baby who was sleeping near by. I told her to just put her mind on Jesus and start praising Him, for it was He who would baptize her in the Holy Spirit. She closed her eyes and started praising the Lord. I too praised Him for what He was about to do. As we prayed I laid my hand on her and asked the Lord to fill her with the Holy Ghost. As we continued to praise the Lord. She began to speak in another language. She was filled with joy and thanksgiving as the power of God filled her being. I praised God for baptizing her with the Holy Ghost.

On another occasion I invited three preteen girls to come to church with me. The girls were first cousins. I had known them all their lives. Their mother was older than I was, but we had all grown up in the same neighborhood. I told them about Jesus and they had a desire to come to church and learn more.

The girls started coming to church regularly. The pastors and members prayed with the girls to receive the Holy Ghost. After spending some time praying and thanking Jesus, they were filled with the Holy Spirit with the evidence of speaking in other tongues.

Not long after the girls received the Holy Spirit their grandmother decided they were going to church too often. She would only let them come once a week. She decided that was too regular, so she stopped them from coming to church.

The pastors and I went to her house to try and persuade her to allow the girls to come to church. She refused saying the girls were too young to become so involved in church. She would not let them come. I felt that my heart would break. I pleaded with her to let the girls come to church. Our plea fell on deaf ears. The girls could not come to church.

The pastors warned the grandmother whose name was Mary, that the Lord would not look kindly on her for hindering the girls from learning about HIM. She ignored the warning.

Some months later, I saw the girls on my way home. I spoke to them. They told me they were going to a party. They said grandmother won't let us come to church, but she lets us go to parties. I told them how much Jesus loved them and encouraged them to pray. Not long after my meeting with them their mother took them and moved up north. I continued to pray for them whenever the Lord brought them to my mind.

Their grandmother was left alone at the house for months. My grandmother who tried keeping a watch over everyone in the neighborhood, asked me if I had seen Ms. Mary, the girls grandmother. I said I hadn't. I haven't seen her in a while she said. Maybe, she went up North to be with her daughter, I said. I don't know, grandma said, I have a bad feeling. Maybe its nothing, I said, you know how private she is.

The next day my grandmother's worrying got the best of her. She went to Ms. Mary's house to find out if she was home. She knocked at the door, but there was no answer. She started asking the other neighbors if they knew if Ms. Mary had gone up north to visit her daughter. Everyone said they didn't know. My grandma wasn't satisfied so she got in touch with Ms. Mary's daughter up north. She found out Ms. Mary was not with her daughter.

Grandma got the police to go with her to Ms. Mary's house, and force open the door to see if Ms. Mary was there, and make sure she was OK.

When they opened the door the stench of rotting flesh greeted them. They looked through the house and found Ms. Mary had died in her bed. Ms. Mary had died alone under horrible conditions, and I felt bad for her. I also believe it is a horrible thing to hinder a child from learing about Jesus.

One of my older brother's friend from high school, and his wife started coming to church with me. After he had been coming to church for a while he told me he wanted to receive the Holy Ghost. I said that's great. At church we prayed with him to receive the Holy Spirit. He found it difficult to focus his thoughts on Jesus. His mind, in his words, kept wandering to other things.

Every Sunday I picked him up for church. I asked him if he were going to receive the Holy Ghost that day. His reply was usually. "I don't know, I'm not sure." I said as long as you are not sure, you will not receive Him, Because the Bible says God wants us to believe before we see any signs.

Finally, he caught on to faith. One Sunday when I went to pick him up, I asked. "Are you going to receive the Holy Ghost today?" He said, "Yes, I am." I smiled in agreement.

When we prayed with him after morning service, he faced the same struggle he had faced at other times, his mind wandered. But this time because he believed God would fill him with his Spirit, he pressed his way past his thoughts. He praised Jesus, and soon he began to speak in other tongues as the Spirit of God gives utterance. He was filled with the Holy Ghost and with power. The Bible says we receive power after the Holy Ghost comes upon us! Thank God for the power of the Holy Ghost.

SCHOOLS

It seemed as if I would never make it, but I graduated from college on time with my BS in Speech Pathology. I had planned to go to graduate school part-time and work a full time job in the fall. That summer proved to be the most exciting summer of my life.

A month or so before school ended I was walking near the married student housing. As I walked I saw a very pretty Latino girl sitting on her porch. She looked very sad. I spoke to her, and we started talking. She told me she had seen me at church. I had not remembered seeing her. I worked with a group that performed plays, so more people saw me than I saw them. However, I always tried to speak to as many people as I could. As we continued to talk, I felt led by the Holy Spirit to share with her. I asked her why she was so sad. At first she tried to pretend I was wrong about her being sad. I said your sadness isn't natural. Jesus makes His people glad.

She began to share with me how her feelings for her husband, a wonderful Jewish brother, had disappeared. She said, I feel nothing for him and he's my husband. I explained to her that God is love and He had the power to cause us to feel love for someone. I told her how the enemy would love to destroy her marriage, but we had the power to stop him. I showed her in the scriptures how precious marriage is to God.

When we finished talking, I told her I was going to pray for her and the Lord was going to renew her love for her husband, and she was going to love him more than she ever had before. I asked her if she believed that. She said she did.

We prayed and asked the Lord to give her love for her husband again. When we finished praying she said I receive whatever God does for me.

She, her husband and I became good friends. I saw her some days later. She and I were driving across town when she began to cry. I stopped the car thinking perhaps she was hurting physically. What's wrong I asked. "I can't help it she said, please I must go back to my house. I turned around and drove back to her house. When we got to her house her husband was in the yard with their son. She jumped out of the car and ran to her husband and said, "I can't explain it, but I feel God, and it's as if He has flooded my heart with love for you. I love you, so much, she cried. The two of them hugged and kissed and cried together. I could not hold back the tears. No one can write a love story like Jesus can. Jesus renewed and restored a marriage the enemy tried to destroy. Praise His Name!

That summer the Lord used the three of us to win souls. We became prayer partners, and decided to share a home when I moved out of the dorms. The wife whom we'll call Issi had a burden for her people in Mexico. We prayed and the Lord blessed us to write and translate a tract in Spanish. We were all newly graduated students, so our finances were low, very low. We took odd jobs to earn extra money to pay for the typesetting and the printing of the tract. It took pooling all of our resources to get the tract done, but the Lord blessed us to do it.

Since we lived in Flagstaff Arizona at the time we weren't far from the Mexican border. We worked and earned money to make the trip.

We went to Mexico and passed out the tracts. The people were so receptive and grateful. When it was time to leave our hearts were sad, but seeing some of the Mexican Christians encouraged us that the new converts had someone to love them through the hard times.

We spent the rest of the summer passing out tracts and telling people about Jesus on our college campus. We continued to do odd jobs during the summer to support ourselves. We were believing God to work out our future.

Toward the end of summer, I was returning home one day, when a lady stopped me and said, "didn't you just graduate?" "Yes,

I did," I said. She went on to say, "I'm a principal, and I wondered if you'd be interested in working at my school?" "My mother told me about you, I've looked at your records, so I know you have a lot of options, but here's my card; I guarantee you a competitive salary." I took her card and headed toward home. Similar situations started happening to everyone in our group. By the time school began, the Lord had blessed all of us with high paying jobs and good benefits. Praise His Name!

Working in Detroit schools was the greatest challenge for me. I started off substituting. My first experience substituting was for a teacher who was pregnant. I was told it was for one day, but when I arrived a woman ran into the office and screamed, "I quit! I can't take those monsters anymore." I was told this was the class I was to take over. I was a little shaken. I had only been teaching for one year.

The principal introduced me to the students, who looked like normal children. The students sat in silence as the principal left and I began the class. One student finished his assignment first and handed me his paper. I said thank-you. He looked at me strange. Before recess was to begin I asked the students to please put their papers and books away.

After recess all the boys in my class were given detention because they were fighting. I spent some time talking to them about anger and how it could destroy a person. One child stood up and said he'd kick anybody's butt in our classroom. I asked him to please sit down. Then another child told me I was weak. I asked why he said that. He said I was weak because I said please and thank-you all the time. I told them I was being courteous and I expected them to say please and thank-you as well. Thus the battle began.

I prayed for the Lord to show me how to reach the children and little by little, day by day I was led. I talked to the children. I was fair with them. I corrected them, and I did the most effective thing a teacher can do I called their parents everytime they acted up. I invited parents to come to visit the classroom unannounced.

They did. They saw their children in the raw. Many were surprised, and rebuked their children for their adverse behavior.

Soon I won the children's respect and their love. I invited them to a young people's Bible study and game night with my minister. They all became regulars at the meeting. They knew I cared and they began to confide in me, and they began to pray.

WHOSE SIDE AM I ON!

A little boy we'll call D. came to me one Friday at the end of class and said, you're always saying Jesus can help everything, can He help me? What do you want Him to do? I asked. Every weekend my mother and my brother get into a fight, and they always put me in the middle and ask me whose side I'm on. I love my mother and I love my brother. I don't know whose side to be on, can Jesus tell me whose side to be on? My heart went out to D. I knew this was really bothering him.

I prayed for God's wisdom. I said listen to me, I want you to do exactly as I tell you to do. If your brother and mother get into a fight this weekend I want you to call on Jesus, you don't have to say it out loud, you can say it in your mind. Just keep saying Jesus. I promise you when you call on Him, He will answer and He will help. There is power in the name of Jesus. I laid hands on the child and I rebuked the fighting in his home and I believed the Lord to work things out.

Monday morning he rushed up to me and said I did what you said and it worked. They started to fight and I called on Jesus in my mind. The next thing I knew my brother stopped talking to my mother, and walked out the house. When he returned he was calm. He and mama were laughing together. Jesus really did help.

I had D. all year. He gave me victory reports all year. They had stopped fighting. He surrendered his life to the Lord. I saw all of the students in that class turn around. The fighting stopped, the cussing stopped, and that class, that was once considered the worse in the school became the most well mannered group in the school. Praise be to the Lord.

A NEW SCHOOL

I was given a permanent assignment the following year in a middle school. We had security guards and policemen at the school. This was a rough school. Most of the students were in a gang or fighting to get in a gang. We had a problem with drugs and drug dealers at the school. On one pay day one student said to one of his teachers, "I bet I have more money than you do; You got paid today, but I bet I have more money than you make in a year." He then took out a fist full of rolled up bills. mostly twenties. It was difficult to encourage the children to get a good education, so they'd get a good job and make good money.

Nonetheless we tried.

ANGER

In this environment I was determined my classroom would be different. My rules were simple in this room we don't cuss, fuss, or fight. There were always those who challenged me, but for the most part all the students complied. The only problem was sometimes their problems got the best of them.

One student we'll call C was filled with anger. One morning he started tossing desks around and threating to beat up another student. I was sitting at my desk at the time. I rushed over to where he was. I said, in the name of Jesus, I rebuke you demon spirit of anger. C flopped down in his chair looking dazed. The anger was gone. I asked him to straighten the chairs. He did. I explained to the class, sometimes we have to cast out evil. News spread around the school that I cast out devils and I had peace in my classroom. While other teachers were filling the office with troubled students I had peace in my classroom because I acknowledged the Lord.

A BATTLE GROUND

Detroit schools were a battle ground at that time, at least one student was shot every week. I watched in the office as six grade students cussed out a parent or hit their parent. I began to talk to my students about honoring their parents as the Bible said. I told them many young people were dying because they did not honor their parents or older people. They listened and they agreed it was important to honor their parents. I saw these children blessed, but my heart went out to the other children I couldn't reach.

I had one student in my class who was very quiet. He stayed by himself. He never bothered anyone and rarely spoke. Another child, we'll call P. picked a fight with him. He told P. to go on. He did, I thought, but as soon I wasn't looking P. was in this boy's face again pushing him.

The boy grabbed P. and was choking him. By now I had called security. I wasn't strong enough to pull them apart, and I couldn't get any of the other big boys to help me pull them apart. All the students were encouraging the fight.

I heard the bones in P's neck begin to crack. I picked up a broom. I told the other big boys if they didn't pull the boys apart, I was going to hit them with the broom. I was not going to stand by and watch that boy break P's neck. They hesitated and then they pulled the boy's arm off of P. P collapsed, but he was all right. Security finally arrived and dealt with the situation. I don't think I would have hit the boys with the broom, but I wanted them to think I would, so they'd help. I think it was God who made them think I would hit them.

I NEED WATER

I had another student in my group who had a hygiene problem. Several students complained to me about his body odor. I tried to be tactful by talking to all the students about good hygiene, and by giving everyone soap, deodorant, and fragrance. This student's odor problem got worse.

After class, one day, I pulled him aside and asked him if he liked the soap, deodorant, and fragrance I'd given him. He said he did. I said you have a body odor what's wrong? He said, "my mama took the money she was suppose to pay the bills with and bought drugs; I don't have any water at my house; We don't have any gas either, so I have to come to school, so I can eat; I'm sorry I smell so bad he said." I was the one who was sorry. I had missed the simplest factor—water.

I made arrangements for the student to take showers at school, before classes began. I made sure he had his things in a separate locker only he had the key to. He didn't have a body odor problem anymore.

LET'S MAKE HER CUSS

Some of the students didn't believe me when I said I didn't cuss. They decided to put me to the test. They had hidden a dead rat under my attendance book in a drawer. Of course, I didn't know anything about this. I came in opened the drawer, grabbed my book and out falls this rat. I screamed Jesus, Jesus, Jesus. It's OK one boy shouted above my voice I'll get rid of it.

I never found out who I should thank for the rat, but one student said to me later, I thought for sure you would cuss and rave. I told him what's in a person will come out of a person. I told him I have Jesus on the inside, so when something upsets me I scream for Jesus. Cussing won't help me. I know Jesus will help me. They didn't test me that way ever again.

HEALED

A NAME GREATER THAN AIDS

At the local church I attended the Pastor assigned me the task of leading the combined choir. I had the opportunity of getting to know all the choir members on a personal basis. One sister in particular comes to mind. For the sake of privacy I'll call this sister "P". P was the quietest sister in the choir, except when she sang. She had a strong lovely voice that could fill a room.

One night at about two in the morning my phone rang. When I answered all I heard was sobbing on the other end. I began to pray. I said its all right; The Lord can handle any problem. After a while a voice spoke and I knew it was P. What's wrong? why are you so sad? I asked. She continued to cry as if her heart was broken. I continued to pray and wait for her to talk to me.

Finally she spoke. My husband, she said, is a mainliner; he used a dirty needle and contracted aids; I went to the doctor today; I'm three months pregnant; the doctor says the baby and I both have aids.

I knew very little about aids, but I knew how deadly it was. I also knew about the power in Jesus name. I knew that no name given under heaven or above heaven was greater than the name of Jesus. I began to share with her the victory we have in Jesus.

I said Jesus has the last word. His Word declares that we are healed by his stripes; there is nothing too hard for the Lord, not even aids; I declare that the baby will be born healthy in JESUS name. I declare that you are completely healed by the power of God.

Do you believe this, I asked her. She stopped crying and she said, yes I receive that, it's the only hope I have.

She received and believed what I said, but everyday until she had the baby she called me for encouragement and revival of her faith. Everyday I preached faith to her and challenged her to believe the Lord and not to accept her situation.

When the baby was born the doctor said the baby had the aids virus. When she called and told me this. I asked her whose report was she going to believe? I said the doctor is a lie, the baby is healed by the power of God.

She took the baby back for the monthly check-up and the doctor said the same thing. The baby has the aids virus. She called me and told me what the doctor had said. I told her the same thing. I said the doctor is a lie the baby is totally healed by the power of God. Don't doubt the Lord I encouraged her.

When the baby went back for the next checkup the doctor repeated the test three times. She said she got worried and asked what the problem was. The doctor told her he'd talk to her after he did the test one more time, and consulted with a colleague of his.

When the doctor spoke with her he said the strangest thing had happened. He said he did the aids test just as he had done it every month prior to this visit, but this time, he said, the test came back negative. He said he ran the test three times himself and his colleague ran the test once and the results were still negative. Your son does not have the aids virus.

P thanked the doctor and told him this is what she had been believing the Lord for. This time when she called me she was overjoyed. He's healed, she shouted, the Lord healed my baby of aids. I rejoiced with her knowing what a great God we serve.

The healing of her baby caused P to have faith to believe God for her healing. She didn't have to call me everyday any more she now had the strength to stand in faith and proclaim "I'm healed by the stripes of Jesus", and so she is.

HE RAISED THE DEAD

Our Pastor felt led to buy a new church, so everyone did what we could to raise money for the new building. We moved into our new building that summer. It was located in a suburban neighborhood. We passed out flyers inviting all the neighbors to join us for church.

That first Sunday in our new building proved to be very exciting. We had a lot of people from the neighborhood come to our service, and we had our regular people there. Everyone was happy and rejoicing in the Lord. When we rejoice in the Lord in our church we dance in the Spirit, we laugh, and we praise the Lord.

One of the deacons was especially happy and thankful to the Lord. He danced all over the church until he collapsed. We always have a nurse on duty during the service. The nurse checked the deacon. She couldn't get a pulse, so she immediately called an ambulance.

The Pastor asked me if I felt any leading from the Lord. I told him I felt the Lord wanted us to just praise Him. He also asked two other ministers in the church how the Lord was leading them. They too felt the Lord was saying praise me for the victory.

We began to softly praise the Lord and thank Him for intervening . I overheard the nurse telling the pastor, the man was turning blue.

The ambulance arrived, and the neighbors who didn't come to the service were definitely at the church when they saw the ambulance. The EMT examined the man and said He had no pulse. They said he was dead, but they did not have the authority to pronounce his death, a doctor had to do that. They asked if the family could give a funeral home where the body could be taken. Someone said they'd contact his mother and she could call them.

We continued to thank the Lord. As we followed the body to the door. I told God in my mind. I said Lord, people are going to think if they come to our church they may fall out and die. Please intervene. As we followed behind the EMTs thanking the Lord for His goodness, and His greatness, when they got to the door, that led outside, the deacon sneezed twice and then a third time. Then he sat up. The EMT s were so startled they dropped the gurney they were carrying him on.

The deacon started praising the Lord even more than he had before. Everyone in the church started rejoicing. The people from outside came in and they saw what had happened, and they started rejoicing too. We rejoiced like never before.

Once again the Lord proved Himself to be more than enough. He proved Himself to be greater than anything we could ever hope for. Jesus is the Lord!

CALLED BY GOD

I was sleeping on the grounds of the Bible school I attended in my car one night when the Lord awakened me. I looked up and the ceiling of the car was gone. I could see the beautiful early morning sky beginning to peek through the night.

The Lord spoke to me. He did not speak in an audible voice. He spoke his words to my mind and spirit. He said "Preach". When He said preach, He took the word preach and put it down inside of me.

How God could speak a "Word", and then take that word and put it in a person is beyond me. I can't explain it, but I know He did it. After musing over this revelation, I fell asleep.

Later that morning I got up and went to the Pastor's house. His wife came to the door. I told her about the vision, saying, I don't understand why God would call me to preach. I don't know enough about Him. I'm so young in the Lord. I don't know my head from my foot so to speak. She smiled at me and said, I can understand why God would call you to the ministry. Then she explained to me that those who minister must wait on their ministering. I had no problem with the waiting part.

I noticed from that day on preaching flowed out of me like water. It was not unusual for me to see a group of people, usually men, standing on a corner, and I stop to tell them about Jesus, and end up preaching a sermon on the street. I'd pray with them and for them. I'd make an altar call right there on the street. I saw the Lord move by His Spirit upon the men. They would cry and repent before the Lord. To me a group gathered on a street corner was an invitation for me to come and preach, and I did.

PRISON MINISTRY

I went to the prisons and jails to tell the women about Jesus. My heart went out to the young girls whose lives were destroyed by drugs and prostitution.

When I first started the Bible class at the county jail about six women attended. The next class we had fourteen women attend the meetings. As usual we sang prayed, taught the "Word", and had an altar call.

When I went for the third Bible class the Captain on duty detained me in his office, and asked me several questions. He wanted to know if I had done any special favors for the girls. I told him I had not. He said I've checked you out, and from everything I can see you are following the rules, more so than others. But I can't understand why every girl in the barrack wants to come to your Bible class. Every girl wants to come I said, we've only had as many as fourteen girls. He said that's the maximum we would let come. Every girl in that barrack has signed up to come to your class. This has never happened before. We can not put you in a room, its too small. I'm going to set you up in the barrack. That's the only way we can accommodate everyone. That's fine with me I said. I had no idea they all wanted to come.

When we went to the barrack, every girl in the barrack was waiting for the Bible class to begin. The Captain and his men set up a table for me up front. We started the meeting with singing and praising God. We had a few testimonies, and I shared the "Word of God". The girls were not allowed to come forward for the altar call for security reasons, so we prayed for needs and salvation from their seats. The Lord moved by His Spirit. Demons were cast out, lives were changed, and souls were reclaimed for Jesus.

The Captain stayed for most of the Bible class. As I was leaving I saw him. He told me he understood why the girls wanted to come to the Bible class. You give them hope, he said. You even gave me hope. He briefly mentioned some things he was going through. I let him know it was and is JESUS who makes the difference, for **HE IS HOPE**

SAVED FROM DEATH

Two girls who were getting out of jail, had no place to go. I had extra room at my house, after praying about the matter, I decided to let them stay at my house. This was temporary until they could get jobs and get their own place.

The girls were grateful for the opportunity. I made it clear that there was to be no smoking, cussing, or drinking in my house before the girls moved in. The girls had sworn off smoking for over sixty days, they said they had no problem with the rules. They said they were Christians and they would live for Jesus.

One of the girls, whom I'll call Ann was very talkative, outgoing, and friendly. During our Bible studies she was always asking questions, and putting the lessons in nutshell messages she could remember. The other girl, whom we'll call Sarah, was quiet and somewhat withdrawn at times, and very outgoing at other times.

Everything was going fine until Ann decided to attend a group session that was similar to an AA group. The lessons taught by the group leader were good. However, Ann started hanging around smokers, and soon she was smoking again. It seemed that before she had a chance to think things over, she was in a relationship with one of the men in the group.

I prayed for her. I told her God's way was marriage first, and sex later. My words fell on deaf ears. For soon she moved in with her boyfriend.

My heart was sad, but I continued to pray for Ann's deliverance. One week I felt a strong leading to pray for God to spare Ann's life. Everyday that week Ann was heavy on my mind. I prayed for her.

Several months had passed since I last saw Ann, and since she was on my mind all that week, I wondered how she was. I was passing the TV set when I heard about a shooting. I hears Ann's name mentioned.

I immediately called the hospital mentioned. They told me Ann was in their care. I rushed to the hospital to see her.

I found out from a newspaper article that Ann had been shot by her friend's boyfriend. When Ann was able to speak, this is what she told me . . .

Her friend's baby's father had come to the house. The friend had hid in a closet in the bedroom when she saw the guy coming. Ann sat on the bed in the bedroom. The man came in the house and walked to the bedroom. He asked Ann where his baby was. She had been told to tell him nothing, so she said she did not know. He asked where his former girlfriend was. Ann said she did not know. The man took out a gun and shot Ann in the head twice, and once in the chest.

Ann said she could not believe she was shot. blood was everywhere. she said she remembered what I said in the Bible class, about Jesus being able to heal anything. She called on Jesus, in her mind, for deliverance. She told the Lord she believed He would heal her.

Someone called an ambulance. When they got her to the hospital, she said she heard the doctor say, "She's wounded too badly, there's no way she'll survive this. Let's just clean up the wounds the best we can. I doubt she'll make it through the night."

Ann said in her mind, Lord the doctors are a lie, and you are truth, and I will live. She said she was conscious for everything, just unable to speak.

To the doctors surprise Ann did live, Praise God. Eventhough she still had one part of a bullet the doctors could not reach in her head, she was talking and chatting as unusual. Granted this was three weeks after her injury.

Ann sat smiling at me with her shaven head saying, this was my wake-up call. I'm going to live for Jesus. I know I should be dead, but He spared my life.

She said after the shooting she had no more desire for smoking at all. The taste was gone. I was so blessed by her testimony of God's faithfulness. I was thankful her life was spared. It turns out the week I felt led to pray for Ann was the week she was shot. The Lord had led me to pray for her three days before she was shot. There is nothing the Lord does not know, and there is nothing He will not do to help us. Praise His Holy Name Forever!

JAPAN

It was in Detroit school system that I was chosen, with other teachers, to learn the Japanese language. Detroit schools began sister state with Shiga in Japan.

I excelled in Japanese. I enjoyed the Language. The more I studied about Japan the more I felt a need to pray for the people. I started out wanting to help send missionaries to Japan. The Lord spoke to my heart about sending me to Japan. I thought it would be through the program in Detroit, but the Lord had other plans.

CHANGING OF THE GUARD

I was in a twelve' O clock prayer meeting in Buffalo NY, almost five years later when the Lord told me this was the year I was to go to Japan. I was meeting with this group everyday at lunch time. Later that week when I met with them, in prayer, the Lord spoke to me and said look up when I looked up I saw what looked like a flash of light. The Lord said this is the angel who will go to Japan with you. Another large flash of light came and I saw the figure of a huge man. A man as round as he was tall. Then he became invisible to me, but I knew he was there.

HELP FROM CHINA

A friend from church heard about a group that was looking for missionaries to go to China. She urged me to call them. I tried to explain I felt led to go to Japan. She continued to urge me to call this group. To please her I called the group. I explained to the man I spoke with I felt led to go to Japan. He said that's interesting you would say that, because my wife works with a group that's looking for missionaries to go to Japan. He said, I'll give her your number.

She called me and we began to put together a program for me to go to Japan. I needed at least ten thousand dollars for the first year. I tried raising the money through donations. I only collected a few hundreds. The money was set up to go directly to the mission. They knew I was not reaching my goal. I had a thousand dollars I could contribute, but everything was just a drop in the bucket.

My contact person with the mission, who we'll call Mrs. J, was concerned. She called me and suggested I set my goal for next year. I told her the Lord said this year. I didn't know how it was going to happen, but I was going to Japan this year.

I began to prepare myself for the trip. I sold or stored everything in my apartment. I even sold my car, and scheduled pick-up of it the week before the group was to leave for California. The plans were to go to the missions headquarters in California for final paperwork, and leave for Japan from there.

My friends thought I was crazy. They came over one night to tell me so. You're not thinking rational, one of them said. You don't have enough money to go to Japan. You've sold everything in your house, another friend, remarked. What happens if you don't go to Japan. You can't live in an empty house, someone said. I believe God,

He said I'm going to Japan this year and I believe that, I said.

I decided to talk with my Pastor again about Japan. Sometimes it takes missionaries years to raise money for a mission overseas, the Pastor said. I'm sure the Lord said this year Pastor, I said. Well, one thing is for sure if the Lord said it, He will do it, he said. I believe that Pastor, I said. I went home and I prayed about my situation again. The Lord again confirmed to me it would be this year, I'd go to Japan.

A week before I was to leave, I still didn't have the money to go. I had something more than money, I had the Word of someone who cannot lie, and someone who will not lie. I had God's Word; I believed Him and that settled it for me. However, I did feel a little nervous when the last week rolled around. I remember telling The Lord the ball is in your court now.

The first part of the last week I received a phone call from Mrs. J. She sounded excited, you won't believe what has happened. Try me, I said. She said, One of the girls, who had raised all her money, decided to get marry; she won't be going; she's donating all her money to you; girl, you must have been doing some tall praying; do you think you can be ready to leave on time she asked. I'm already packed, all I need is my ticket, I said. I trusted the Lord and He gave me more than enough money to go to Japan. The Lord keeps His Word, we have no reason to doubt Him.

THE FIRST YEAR IN JAPAN

My first year in Japan was exciting. We passed out tracts, taught English and saw many Japanese people come to the Lord. I was bothered though when I saw that many of the new converts would still frequent the temples where idol worship took place.

One of my older students put it best when she said, "I don't want to offend any gods, so I worship them all". This was the thinking of many Japanese people, until they received the Holy Ghost. When they received the Holy Ghost they understood the fact, there is only one God who sent His son into the world because of His great love for us. The Spirit filled Japanese worshipped the one true God and His son Jesus.

I made it a point to share with the Japanese people the baptism in the Spirit. The first church I was assigned to was not a Spirit-filled church. When we arrived at the church two of the members pulled me aside and said, you're Spirit-filled aren't you. Yes, I replied. We have been praying for you to come, when we saw you we knew you were Spirit-filled like us, they said. I felt blessed by them.

The Lord blessed me to help the church in many ways. The Japanese pastor told me I was a "real missionary". Coming from him that was a lot. He listened intently to everything I had to say about the Spirit baptism, in the end he said, "Jenny, you almost persuaded me, but my church believes differently, and I must agree with them."

Months later when I was working with another church I remember him sending for me to cast the devil out of a woman who was demon possessed. My heart went out to him because he didn't have the power of God on the inside, who would give him the confidence he needed to cast out devils and do great things for the Lord.

THE ACCURSED THING

One of my older students said she would come to church with me if I went to the temple garden with her. I agreed. All the temple gardens are beautiful parks where many tourist frequent. However, all of the gardens are dedicated to demons. In Japanese most of the signs say, "may the demons who dwell here bless you" . But the problem is demons can't bless us, only the Lord God can bless us.

The day before I went to the park I prayed and talked to the Lord about it. The Lord told me not to buy or eat anything in that place, because it was accursed.

We went to the park. Where ever I walked I claimed the land for Jesus. My student stopped to pray at a well. When she finished she asked me if I would pray. I told her I did not pray to idols made by men, I prayed to the one true God, the only living God.

She said oh yes, you mean Jesus and God. I pray to them too. I don't won't to make any of them mad. I told her the Lord was the only Lord. He is not just one of the gods. I told her Jesus said I am the way which means there is only one way to get to God, and that is through Jesus. I told her how much Jesus loved her and wanted to save her.

She listened intently. She told me that sometimes she got tired of having to pay the priest for everything they did and how she would like to feel peace in the midst of her troubles. She said she'd think about what I said.

Before we left the park my student took me to see a new addition to the park. It was a history of the past rulers in Japan. It was each ruler's story told with clothing and artifacts from their era. I was given an English tract as I entered the hall. It was an intresting exhibit. After we had toured the entire exhibit my student and I said our goodbyes and departed for home.

Later that night when I retired I had trouble sleeping. This was unsual for me, I usually fell asleep shortly after retiring. I felt like a person would feel if they were being tormented by mosquitoes. I felt annoyed. I prayed. The Lord reminded me of and led me to read the story of AI in the Bible.

In this story when Joshua and his troops should have met with success in conquoring a small village, they were defeated. When Joshua inquired of the Lord as to why they were defeated, as to why He did not give them victory over their enemy; The Lord told them He did not give them victory because they took of the accursed thing. In Joshua 6 (Kings James Version of the Bible)

God had instructed Joshua to tell the people to not take anything from the city of Jerico when they destroyed it, because it was accursed. In Jericho at that time the people worshipped many false gods. This is abhorred in the eyes of the true and living God. It is also abhorred by all who worship the true and living God. God hates idol worship, He does not want His people bowing down to gods made of stone or wood, or worshipping angels or stars or the like.However, one of Joshua's men saw something he liked and he took it and hid it in his tent.

Because of this man's disobediance thirty-six men from the tribe of Israel lost their lives in battle. Thus Joshua inquired of the Lord. The Lord told Joshua which one of his men disobeyed when he inquired. For his disobediance this man and his entire family was punished with death.

When I asked the Lord how this story related to me, He said I too had taken of the accursed thing. I said no Lord, I did not eat, drink or buy in that place. The Lord asked, what is that in your coat pocket? I looked in my coat pocket, and I found the English tract I had been given by the matron at the King's exhibit. I had absentmindedly placed the tract in my pocket without thinking. I had taken of the accursed thing.

I asked the Lord to forgive me for my disobediance. I took the tract and I burned it. You see the paper itself was not evil, but because it came from a place where idol worship occurs, and false gods are bowed down too, the paper just like everything in Jericho was contaminated. The Lord forgave me and I learned a vaulable lesson. I rebuked the tormenting spirits that were allowed to come in because I had the tract. I retired to a peaceful night sleep.

That Sunday, my student came to church with me as she had promised. When the invitation was made she later went foward for prayer, because she said she wanted peace.I praise God that He is the giver of peace. I praise God that He alone is the only true God, and that Jesus His son is the anointed Messiah of the world. Amen.

STAY IN JAPAN.

I was only scheduled to spent a year in Japan. However, the Lord said I was to stay in Japan. How long I didn't know. To stay in Japan one needed a sponsor. Someone to say I assume responsibility for this person and I will pay their fare home when they decide to return to their country. The sponsor had to be Japanese.

The mission I was with had limited sponsorship ability and had to schedule people a year to two years ahead. They could not sponsor me. I knew the Lord said stay. I waited on His next move.

A JOB

The next move came sometime later when I was taking the train home from a church meeting. I saw a man, his wife and their two little boys. The man looked like a farmer from Holland. Since I rarely met Americans, I assumed he was from Holland. His little boy started playing a game of hide and seek with me. Hiding behind his father. The father noticed him and said, I see you've found a new friend. You're from America, I said excited to meet other Americans. We started talking and soon realized we had gone to the same university, with the exception he was older than myself. We had also graduated in the same field of study.

While we were talking the Holy Ghost spoke to me and said this man was to help me find a job. I said to the man, I know you're going to think this is a little strange, but the Lord just said you are going to help me find a job. "Me, God said I'm going to help you find a job; I don't know of anything; are you sure God said that?" Listen, I said, here's my name, address, and phone number, when the Lord shows you whatever it is He has for me, please call me or write. I had reached my stop so I got off. I waved goodbye to the couple and the boys. I could see the worried look on the husband's face. I prayed for him.

In the weeks that followed that man sent me every ad he could get his hands on. With every clipping he asked are you sure God said that? I wrote him back and said, please don't send me any more ads; don't do anything just relax; whatever God has for me He will show it to you and you will know it's for me. The ads stopped coming.

A week before it was time for me to move I received a call from the man. You're not going to believe this, he said, a school I worked at five years ago when I first came to Japan, called me and asked me if I knew anyone who could teach English at their school; guess who came to mind; a black lady on a train who said, the Lord said, you're going to help me find a job. We both rejoiced.

I interviewed with the school personnel, and was hired. I worked with that school until I left Japan.

THE APARTMENT

My new school was located outside of Tokyo, in an area called Kofu which was in Yamanashi. I was only about an hour's drive from Mt. Fuji, Japan's famous volcano. When I arrived in Kofu I had to find housing. In Japan one must pay a deposit, first month's rent, and a gift amount to the landlord which equals a month's rent for allowing one to stay in their apartment. Most apartments ran one thousand dollars or more a month. I did not have this amount of money.

I had been told all the landlords in Japan expected their money before one could move in. I prayed and I believed the Lord would make a way for me. In Japan it's always better to let someone who knows the person do the talking. I prayed as the former teacher explained my situation to the landlord. The landlord explained to the teacher, what I was asking was unheard of in Japan, but she said, "I had a dream that makes me feel, I am suppose to help her". She opened the door to me. I was allowed to pay her when I received my first check, the school had decided to pay the deposits. The Lord did it again.

We take for granted little things such as sheets blankets, beds, pots and pans. All the little necessities which I did not have. I prayed for the Lord to open a door. Trying to buy all these things new was out of the question.

Everything in Japan was expensive. A cup of coffee cost five dollars. That was the price at reasonable places, more expensive places charged more. In Japan, there were no thrift stores, or Walmart. I needed a miracle.

A lady from one of the nearby churches I'd be working with came to see me. I want to help, she said, what do you need? I told her everything I needed. She took my needs to the church. The next day she and a few others brought bedding, chopsticks, a pot and pan and some other things needed for daily living. I was so thankful and so blessed. The Lord had done it again.

UNIVERSITY CONCERT

The second week I was in Kofu I passed a university and the Holy Ghost said to me I was to have a concert there to draw the young people in; the concert was to take place in two weeks. I told the Japanese Christians the Lord said, I'm to have a concert at that university in two weeks. They all looked at me and laughed. Oh no sister, this is not America. To have a concert at that university one must plan at least a year ahead, then it will take six months to plan for the actual event, the Japanese pastor told me.

Can we ask the university and see what they say, I asked. It would be embarrassing, they will say no, replied a church member. I believe the Lord spoke to me. If the Lord did not speak to me, then the university will refuse my request, however, if the Lord in deed spoke to me, then the university will grant my request. After three hours of debating among themselves the Japanese church members agreed to ask the university about the concert.

One of the church members who was a professor went to the university with my request. He returned with their answer the next night. I was shocked, he said, a Christian group of young people heard my request and said they would sponsor Jenny and her group. They had been praying for an event they could sponsor that would reach out to the students. The answer was yes.

Japanese people are great planners, as long as they know all the details. God on the other hand does not always give all the details at one time. I knew I was going to sing and I knew some other people were to help me, but I didn't know who they were. When I shared this information with the Japanese church, they were not to happy. I assured them the Lord would work out the details.

I sang at a church in Tokyo twice a month with some Christians from Hawaii. I had thought they were to help me, but the Lord said no. This particular weekend when I was there the pastor introduced a "Youth with a Mission" (YWAM) group. They were twelve young people from different parts of the world. They would be helping at the church for two weeks. The Lord said, they were to help me. I spoke with the pastor and their team leader who both agreed it was a great opportunity to witness.

Now the only problem was getting all of them to Kofu, our prefecture or district. Train fare was very expensive. I told the church of my desires. They agreed train fare was not the answer. They finally agreed to pay bus fare for the group since bus fare was a little more reasonable. The arrangements were made and the plans were set.

On the day of the concert, the YWAM group arrived that morning. we passed out gospel tracts and flyers about the concert which would be held that night. We were also serving food afterwards for the students. The Japanese students were happy to meet students from so many different countries at one time. They were very receptive.

That night we sang, we did skits, and we presented the gospel to the students who came to the concert. Many came out of curiosity, and many stayed out of curiosity. It was past midnight when we finished eating and said our good-byes to the students. The souls the Lord wanted to draw He drew. The joy came when the students kept their word and we saw them in church that Sunday morning. The Word of the Lord does not go out void.

I saw many souls filled with they Holy Ghost speaking in tongues in Japan, but the strangest thing to me was to hear a Japanese person who did not know English receive the Holy Ghost and start speaking in English. That was a treat God let me witness.

EARTHQUAKES

Japan was prone to earthquakes. The first time I experienced or heard of an earthquake was in my apartment. It was evening. I was relaxing. I heard something that sounded like a huge truck passing by on my street. That wasn't so unusual, the streets in Japan were small, and when a large truck went by it shook things a bit.

A short time later the neighbor from upstairs banged on my door. Are you all right, he said, as I opened the door. Of course, what's wrong I answered. The earthquake, he yelled, it was pretty bad. There was no earthquake I said. He looked at my apartment in amazement. I thought maybe the guy was imaging things.

By now the land lady had come over too. I know this was your first earthquake, she said, are you all right? I'm fine, I said, a little puzzled by now. Come I'll show you, said my neighbor The landlord and I walked upstairs to the apartment directly above me. It was in shambles, everything had been turned upside down. What happened? I said. The earthquake did this said the neighbor. But I didn't feel an earthquake I said.

Now the Landlord was puzzled. She and the neighbor walked back with me to my apartment. They saw everything was in order. By now everybody was standing outside and the upstairs neighbor was showing them my apartment. I in turn was looking at their apartments in amazement. They were all in shambles, everything was overturned.

Why were you spared, asked the landlord? The God I serve, the one true God spared me I said. They all looked at me strange, but that Sunday they decided they had better come and check out the God who saves from earthquakes.

The second time I experienced an earthquake was when I was on the military base. This time I was at a friend's house with another friend who was visiting for the weekend. My friend was down the street at the recreation center working with a group of young people. She rushed in and asked if we were all right. We're fine I said, what's wrong? There was an earthquake, the rec. center is a mess, thank God the kids just had minor scratches, she said.

Are you serious I asked. Looking around her house, she said, that's strange nothing is moved here. We had an earthquake, come on I'll show you. we walked to the rec. center with her and sure enough the whole place was a mess. pool table overturned, piano upturned and toys and cabinets everywhere. All around the area people were reporting the same type of tragedy. My friend said, maybe you are the girl who God doesn't allow to feel earthquakes.

I lived in Japan for three years and they had several earthquakes, which I read about in the paper, measuring from 7.0 on the R. Scale, but I never felt one of them or experienced their effect. I think I didn't feel them because of the angel, the Lord sent with me to Japan.

WITNESSING

We witnessed and did concerts in the park and drew thousands to hear the gospel. In Japan it isn't hard to draw a crowd. There are so many people there. In Tokyo I walked on a sidewalk with three-four hundred or more people at a time. The city is truly populated.

Many people would come to a concert and listen to us speak, but getting them to commit was very difficult; but that was God's job; all we had to do was tell them, and disciple them when they came. We did.

THE COFFEE HOUSE

A friend of mine was helping another group open what I thought was a Christian coffeehouse. He invited me to sing there on the opening night. The day before I was to go to Tokyo to sing, I had a dream. I dreamt I was singing and a drunk man heard my song. When the man left the bar, my song followed him home. I woke up. I had no desire to sing at a bar. I thought, what a strange dream.

I went to the coffeehouse the next evening. I sang and shared the Word and shared my testimony of God's deliverance. When I finished singing I remember telling one of the people from church, some of the people really looked drunk. Before she could answer me, a Japanese man came up to me, and began to tell me how much he enjoyed my singing. He was drunk and his breath nearly knocked me out. That's nice I said, turning back to my friend. He's drunk, I whispered. What's going on here. This is a bar, didn't you know? She asked.

I spoke with the guy who invited me and asked why he didn't tell me it was a bar when he invited me. I thought you wouldn't come if I told you, and these people need to hear about Jesus too. He was right, I probably would not have come if I knew it was a bar; as I looked around I realized these people really did need to hear about Jesus. I had done all I felt the Lord wanted me to do, so I left.

Two Sundays later I was at the Tokyo church and the man who had said he liked my singing was at church. He rushed up to me, and said, your singing followed me home. He called to his family, and said, here she is, this is the girl who sang the songs that followed me home. He told me he came to church the Sunday after the meeting at the bar, and every Sunday since then he's been bringing various family members with him. I was so happy to see he had decided to follow Jesus. It was exceptional that this man had persuaded various family members to come to church with him. In Japan, most families disown family members who become Christians and treat them as if they are traitors.

Romania

A Japanese friend and I felt led to go and help at an orphanage for children in Romania. The country side in Romania was beautiful. A French team was also coming the same time we were. The Lord blessed me to share with the French group, who was very interested in the miracles I'd seen God do, The more I shared the more they wanted me to share. They were hungry for God.

When we arrived at the orphanage the children were so happy to see us. They stared at me for a very long time because they had only seen one other black person before, he was from Russia, I was told. There were also two black girls on the French team. They got their share of stares too.

Most of the children spoke perfect English. Most of them had been in the orphanage since they were a baby. Their caregivers were Americans. All of the children were little sweethearts.

Living at the orphanage was different. It took a while to get use to having soup everyday with a little piece of cabbage and potato in it, but no meat. Meat was something the rich people ate in Romania. Washing a ton of dishes every evening by hand also took getting use to. I was glad we rotated the chores. My favorite assignment was helping the small children get to bed. I loved listening to them pray before retiring. The children were only two to five years old, but when they prayed they sounded like grownups who had walked with God for many years. They prayed about everything and everyone that was on their minds.

I listened as one child said, Dear Lord, help B. he has not been feeling well, heal him. We know you can do it. When one child was sick and present, the children would lay hands on that child and pray. The child would be healed.

VANILLA/CHOCOLATE

The children directed most of their questions to me since the other black girls spoke limited English. One morning, two fourth grade boys conducted a conversation for my listening pleasure. They stood in earshot and began to talk:

A: I think she is a white person who just stayed in the sun too long.
B: I don't know.
A: I'm sure that's what happened, that's why they tell us not to stay in the sun too long.
B: Maybe, but I don't know.

I saw them glancing my way waiting for me to solve the dilemma. I obliged. I didn't stay in the sun too long, I said. I was born this color, this is the way God made me, just like He made you that color, I ended. God made you that color said one boy. Yes, He did, and I love it. I like my color too he said. Then the three of us ran off to play ball together.

Another time I was sitting on the fence with a four year old, he asked, do you taste like chocolate? nope, do you taste like vanilla? I asked. He licked his arm, and replied, nope. That was the end of the questions about color.

We took turns sharing Bible lessons with the children. It was a joy to spend time with them. I believe the Lord is going to use those children to evangelize their country. Romania is a poor country. In our section, the orphanage was the only house with running water, and electricity.

One day the children invited me to go swimming with them. I asked where they swam at. They pointed to a creek not far from the house. Is that the same creek animals and people bathe in I asked. Uh mm, replied a small child. One day, while I was swimming, a boy said, horse manure came floating down the creek from the horse upstream. Well, I don't think I have time to go swimming today I said. Off the children ran to the creek.

GOD SENT YOU

I was walking in the neighborhood, with two friends, when a lady approached me. I know God sent you, she said, I can see God's light in you. She took me by the hand and said, come with me to meet my friend. I was glad my friends came along too.

It was almost dark. Dark in Romania was dark. There were no street lights. She led us to a small hut. We went inside. There was a woman in bed. As best she could the woman in bed told us what was wrong with her. My friend who spoke Romanian was very limited and the other woman only spoke a little English. Somehow God went passed the barrier. Let's pray, I said. My friends and I laid hands on the woman's chest and prayed.

She got up out of the bed and started calling her family members from the other room. When they came in she told them something in Romanian. Then they came and stood in front of us and placed our hands on them for prayer. We prayed for all of them. We prayed for a young boy who had an open wound on his leg. A young woman had a lump or something in her breast which she unashamedly raised her blouse to show me. We prayed. The Lord gave great deliverance to that family.

They came to church Sunday, and testified of God's deliverance in their bodies. This time we had an interpreter. The older woman on the bed had a heart condition and said she could not get up, but the Lord healed her; the young boy had hurt his leg on a fence; the young woman had a lump in her breast. They were all healed by the power of God.

HOME AGAIN

I was allowed to teach Bible stories at a child care center for children ages two to five. One day I shared the story of Jesus healing the lame man. One little girl asked, can Jesus still heal people today? Yes, He can, I said. I didn't think anymore about the lesson or the question. I continued to share stories of Jesus healing people.

One morning, a parent walked up to me and said, my daughter healed her sister this weekend. She said you taught her to do this. I did, I said, completely caught off guard. She told me the story. Her youngest daughter who was three came to her mother complaining of a headache. The mother said the child had headaches before, but she always waited for the second complaint before giving her medicine. When the child did not return the mother went to the bedroom to check on her. When she got to the bedroom door she saw the four year old sister laying hands on the three year old saying, "in the name of Jesus be healed." Then they returned to playing. The mother decided she'd wait to see if the child complained again. After an hour of waiting, the mother asked the child how was her head. She said Jesus healed me.

Another time at the same center. One five year old was going to have to lose his turn at setting the table because he had a bad cold. He stood before me with heavy green mucous flowing from his nose saying, please let me set the table. Not today, we have to wait until you're better, I said as I wiped his nose. One little girl who was standing nearby said, maybe Jesus will heal you. The little boy looked at me and said, will you pray for Jesus to heal me. I prayed. The little boy said, when Jesus heals me can I set the table then. I said yes, but you must wait until He takes away all the nose running and the fever. He went and sat in the hall with the other children.

It was morning, we still had a few minutes before it was time to set the table before lunch. When it was time to set the table, The boy ran up to me and said, Jesus healed me, can I set the tables now. I felt his head, his fever was gone, and his nose which was running all morning was completely dried up and clear. Amazed at how quickly he was healed I said, all right go wash up to set the tables. The child's mother was also amazed to have dropped off a sick child, and was now picking up a completely healed child.

YOU WILL RECOVER ALL

I was taking graduate classes after school. I taught at an elementary school. this particular day I had to get my car repaired. the previous day I had taken several hundreds from my checking account to pay for the repair. The shop manager preferred cash for major work. when school was out the principal called a special mandatory meeting. I had to reschedule my repair job.

After the meeting, I had to rush to get to class on time. when class ended a girl came up to me and asked if I had change for the pay phone. I looked in my coin purse where I had stuffed the hundreds I had for car repair. I gave her coins, and I thought no more about it.

On the way home I stopped at a local market to pick-up a few things I needed. I got ready to pay for my food, and I could not find my coin purse. It was gone, and the hundreds I had for car repairs were gone with it.

I rushed back to the school, thinking I had dropped the purse, and I searched for it. I couldn't find the purse. I reported the loss to the campus police. The police informed me that I could say goodbye to my money because it would not be returned.

I was so worried I went home and called a friend who lived near the school and asked if he would go to the school with me, and help me look for my purse. My friend came to pick me up. As we were going out the door, the Lord spoke to me. He said, you've done everything else why not pray. I told my friend I wanted to pray before I went to look. We prayed. when I prayed the Lord spoke to me, and said, "you shall recover all".

We went to look for the purse. It was hard to see anything in the dark. We didn't find my purse. My friend took me home.

I fell asleep. As I was waking from sleep I had a vision. In the vision I saw a student pick-up my purse, open it, and look at the money. I spoke out loud, "In Jesus Name you cannot have that money, you must return it. It is not yours, and you must return it. I awoke saying these words.

Three days past and everyday I had the same vision and I spoke the same words. Everyday, I checked with the campus police to see if my purse had been turned in. I got the same answer everyday, "No your purse was not turned in. Ms. people don't usually turn money in. That may be true I said, but the Lord said I'd get my money back, and I believe Him.

Early Monday morning, the Lord woke me up and said, go get your money. I said from where. It's at the police station, He said. I went to the police station and asked if they had found my purse. This time they said they would check with the captain. The captain came out and asked me questions about my purse and its contents which I answered. Then he said, the strangest thing happened earlier this morning; A young guy came in with this purse and said he found it. I asked, who was he, I'd like to reward him. He didn't leave his name, the captain said, he said he just wanted to return the purse before something bad happened to him; he said he knew he was not to touch the money in this purse. I thanked the captain and reclaimed my purse. Everything was in it, even the vitamin, I had forgotten to take. Praise God! I recovered all.

FREED FROM OPPRESSION

As a teacher, one encounters all types of problems and all types of people who must be dealt with in various ways. One such problem arose from within the church and the school. I had been appointed choir director at my church. One of the ladies in my group expressed concern for her fourteen years old daughter who constantly ran away from home. Since the girl went to the school where I taught, the mother had asked me if I could talk to the daughter and encourage her not to run away.

I met with the girl a few days later. I told her how dangerous it was to run into the streets at night, and how someone could take her and no one would know where she was. The child listened to me, and she agreed that if she felt the need to leave home she would run to a friend's house, but she would not promise that she would not run away. I asked our school counselor to talk to the child. She refused to talk to the counselor. She continued to run away from home, but she kept her word. She ran to friend's homes.

A few weeks later this girl's younger sister was transferred to my classroom. I suspected something was very wrong at home if the older child felt a need to run away. I continued to pray for the family.

One day the mother's car broke down, and she needed to go to the grocery store. She asked me if I could take her to the store. I agreed, and I met her that Saturday morning. We went to the store and returned. I was helping her carry bags inside. I walked up to the door, and the mother yelled, go on inside. When I went inside I saw the father leaned over the younger child who was lying on the couch. I assumed the child was hurt. Is everything OK I asked. As soon as they realized my presence, the younger daughter jumped up from the couch. She looked embarrassed, and I wasn't sure why. Are you OK I asked again. I thought you were hurt when I saw your father leaning over you. oh, she said, daddy was just playing around. Then, you're not hurt. No, she said, and turned toward me. When she turned toward me I saw a huge bruise mark on her neck. She was a very fair girl, so the mark stood out. Oh my God, you are hurt, I gasped. No, she said, I'm not hurt. But how did you get the bruise, I asked. Daddy did it she replied. Did you fall accidentally, I asked. No, she said Daddy sucked it. Now I understood why the older child ran away from home. I wanted to help in anyway I could. I wanted the children safe.

I spoke with the mother and asked her if the husband sexually abused the girls. The mother assured me this was not the case.

The children's grandmother came from England to visit them. The grandmother saw me at church, and said, she heard I was asking questions about abuse in the home and wanted to talk to me. I scheduled to meet with her, but she canceled the appointment. Later I discovered the grandmother had been told by the parents that she could not talk to me if she wanted to continue to stay at their house.

One day at school the younger daughter was having trouble in the classroom. I took her outside the room to speak to her and calm her down. She had gotten into a heated argument with another student. As I concluded my talk with her I said, if there is ever a time you want to talk to someone about what's going on at your house, I'm here for you. I want to see you safe. The Lord wants to see you safe. Jesus loves you. The little twelve years old looked at me and said, I can't tell you what's happening at my house. Everyone will get mad at me, and I'll get into trouble. I tried to explain to her that she would not get into trouble, and no one had the right to hurt her or touch her in anyway she didn't want to be touched.

The child started to cry. I'll protect you I said, I won't let anything happen to you. You are so special to the Lord, He loves you so much.

The girl told me how her father was sexually abusing her sister. Later, I found out the father had attacked the twelve years old the night before. She had been too ashamed to tell me. I took the information to the school counselor. The counselor called the girls to the office and spoke with both of them. With tears and sobbing the girls told their story.

The father came to pick the girls up from school. When he came to the school, the policemen arrested him.

When the mother found out what had happened, she came to my house and told me I had signed her death warrant. He'll be out she said, and he'll try to kill me. She left screaming I hate you for doing this.

The grandmother also came to see me. She said I thank God for you. You saved this man's life. She said, I had placed this knife under my pillow; I had said in my heart that the next time that man touched my granddaughter I would cut his throat. The Lord used you to save his life. She thanked me for what I had done.

Before the trial, the girls called me to say their mother was telling them if they did not drop the charges against their father, they would have to move out. They wanted to know if they could come to my house to stay.

I went over to talk to the mother. The Lord has brought a great deliverance in the lives of your daughters. You should be happy for them, I said; They are free and so are you. I will take them home with me if I have too, but I would much rather they stayed with you, and see what it's like to live in a home free of abuse. They love you I said and they want to be with you. you're their mother. She listened to me and agreed the girls could stay with her.

At the trial the father received the maximum sentence a child abuser could get. He would be in prison until all the children were grown up and on their own.

Later when I saw the children their countenance looked different. They were in counseling and they were covered in prayer. The youngest girl came up to me and said, I feel like you're my mom, because you didn't stop until I was safe. Thank-you.

The lord moves in mysterious ways his wonders to perform. A lady I once knew said she asked the Lord why were child abusers allowed to get away. She said the Lord told her that there was always someone who knew about the child being abused, but they didn't always tell anyone about the abuse. I am so glad the Lord gave me the mind to tell someone about the children I saw who were being abused. Praises to the Lord Almighty.

IN THE NAME OF JESUS

The Rapist

I joined an early morning group of walkers who lived in my neighborhood. Every morning before work we would walk and run for at least 2-4 miles. Part of our route took us through a small part of downtown.

The third day of running I sprang my ankle and had to walk the full route the next day. One of the girls decided to walk with me as the others ran ahead. As we walked we talked and laughed.

Suddenly from out of nowhere we saw a very tall man standing in front of one of the stores we had to pass by. I tried to tell my friend to move over so we'd be on the street, and not on the sidewalk which would put some distance between myself and the man. As I whispered to my friend to move over, she was whispering to me that she had read in a book, that if we look an attacker in the eye we might be able to scare him off. Please move over I whispered. We can't show fear, she said, I have my key and we can use that as a weapon. That guy is over six feet tall, I whispered, move over.

By now we were upon the man. As we walked past him, he reached out and grabbed me in my chest. When he grabbed me I screamed, JESUS, as loud as I could. When I screamed Jesus the man let me go. I ran one way and he ran the other way. My key holding friend had already run and returned with the others.

I believe if I hadn't known to call on Jesus I would have been raped and possibly hurt or killed. I praise God that demons tremble at the sound of that name JESUS.

IN THE NAME OF JESUS

No More Fear

I met my twelve years old brother one day after school, and I noticed that he looked really fatigued. What's wrong I asked, you look so stressed out. I'm having trouble sleeping at night he said; I fall asleep and then late at night when everyone else is asleep I am awakened; I can't explain it, but I feel an evil presence in the room; I feel so afraid until I can't get to sleep. How long has this been going on I asked. I haven't been able to sleep all week, he said.

Listen to me, I said, I'm going to pray with you, and the next time you are awakened I want you to close your eyes and just start saying Jesus. Keep saying Jesus until the fear leaves. We prayed and he went home.

The next day when I saw my brother he was so excited. I did what you said. When I was awakened I started calling on the name of Jesus. When I called on Jesus the whole room lit up and I felt so much peace. The evil presence just left. I was able to get a good night sleep. I felt so much peace. Jesus is real and He has all power. Amen Amen!

EASTER MORN.

My friend invited me to stay overnight at her house and go to church with her family for sunrise services. This would be my first sunrise service after receiving the Holy Ghost. I was very excited about the service. I was also afraid I might oversleep. I told the Lord about my fear of oversleeping before I went to bed that night, and I asked Him to please wake me on time.

The next morning I was awakened by a bright light shinning in my face. It felt like sunlight. In the depth of my sleep I could hear someone gently saying time to get up. The sunlight got brighter, and I realized it must be midday or later. I jumped out of bed thinking I had awakened too late for church. I was surprised to see the room was completely dark and void of windows. There were no windows in this basement room.

The son had come to wake me so I would be on time for church. What a blessing! We had a great time in church that Easter morning. Truly the son had risen in my life.

MISSION WORK ABROAD

France

My Japanese friend and I stopped in France to visit friends before returning home. The pastor we visited asked us to share with some of his members that evening at a dinner held in our honor. The Lord told me to tell them about the Holy Ghost baptism. I shared with them about the Holy Spirit. When I finished they sat in silence and looked at me. Then they began to ask question after question about the Holy Spirit baptism. The pastor told me later that he had been planning to talk to his group about the Holy Spirit, but wasn't sure how to approach the subject. He said only God could have told me to share about that.

I was surprised this congregation knew so little about the Holy Spirit. Many of them told me they were going to go home and research information about the Holy Spirit. They thanked me for sharing. I was hoping some of them would get filled with the Holy Ghost that night, but the Lord has his time when He'll fill them. In the meantime He used us to plant a seed.

Austria

We visited and shared at a Bible Study in Austria. I felt led to share about having boldness to witness and be a witness. These German speaking Christians listened intently as I spoke through an interpreter. When I finished different ones came forward for prayer. Several of them confessed that eventhough, they had the Holy

Ghost they found themselves drawing back and quenching the Spirit. We began to bind the Spirit of fear and doubt. When we finished we were all revived and ready to go out and win the world for Jesus. The Lord also healed many sick bodies that night. We had an old fashioned revival meeting. Praise God!

PHILIPPINES

We traveled to the Philippines to share Jesus. Once again we found souls hungry for the Word and for the power of God. We preached, sang and demonstrated the power of God. We saw bodies healed and demons cast out by the power of God. I wondered why we didn't see more miracles in more developed countries. Looking at the meager surroundings in the Islands, I understood why they had so much faith, they had to hope for more.

A LADY HEALED IN JESUS NAME

A lady came to one of our churches in Buffalo NY. She sat in the back of the church. The service was scheduled to start in a few minutes. One minister noticed the lady was crying. She went to her and inquired what was wrong. She told the minister she had come the night before, for prayer for her mother. Today at the hospital the doctor told her, the mother had taken a turn for the worse and was dying.

The minister called the group together. She said we are going to pray for this sister's mother; I want everyone to do exactly as I say. She asked everyone to go outside and face in the direction of the hospital. The hospital was several miles from the church. Everyone obeyed. She then asked the people to say what she said. She began to call the mother by name commanding her to get up in Jesus' name; declaring she was healed in Jesus' name. The church was located on a busy street, there were several onlookers, in cars and on feet. Some who laughed and mocked when the church people pointed toward the hospital and declared the woman healed.

When she finished the minister led everyone inside, to start the meeting for the evening. The daughter returned to the hospital to check on her mother. When she got there several nurses were around her mother's room. She ran to her mother's room, asking what was wrong. Several nurses at the door said she couldn't go in right now. That's my mother in there she said, as she pushed past the nurses.

When she got inside she saw her mother pulling the tubes out of her body, saying I'm healed I heard them call my name, they said I'm healed in Jesus name. As soon as the mother pulled a tube out, the nurses would put it back in. The daughter stopped them and told them she believed her mother was healed. That woman walked out of that hospital room totally healed in Jesus' name.

SET FREE

I had a teaching contract in Arkansas. I worked there for about four years as a speech pathologist. My first year, at one of the three schools I was assigned to, was a little rocky. I was amazed at the way the Lord turned situations around. A student was sent to my class one morning. I was working with two other students, at the time. I asked the student to return to his classroom and return at his scheduled time. He obeyed, but he was back in five minutes. When I asked him why he came back. He said, I told the teacher it's not time for me to come to speech, but she insisted I come anyway. Please return to your room and tell your teacher I cannot see you now. I have students. The third grader left again.

In a few minutes he returned with the teacher. I went into the hallway to talk with her. She was very angry. I spoke calmly hoping to calm her. She said this student is suppose to have speech now. I gave you a copy of the new schedule remember, I said. I explained the reason for changing the schedule, and we've been on this schedule for over a month now. She shook her finger in my face and said, I said he's coming to speech now. I said, I'm sorry I have a group now, and turned to close my door. The teacher grabbed the door and pulled; I looked her in the eye and said, in the name of Jesus, you demon spirit of anger, I command you to come out. She let go of the door and walked away without saying a word.

I explained to the students who were watching, anticipating a fight, If I didn't know Jesus maybe I would physically fight, but I know Jesus and I fight with His weapons. I explained the woman had a lot of anger. Yeah, said a student, she was really mad. I helped her by casting out the spirit of anger, now she can think and not just react.

News spread quickly around the school. The buzz was Ms. King cast the devil out of Ms. C. One teacher told me the situation was even discussed at a teacher's meeting saying, the principle said I should cast the devil out of a few more teachers.

Ms. C stopped by my room after school. She said she wanted to apologize for being so angry. She went on to say, you didn't have to call me a name though. What name did I call you, I asked. You called me a demon, she said. Oh no, I didn't call you a demon. I said, remember when you grabbed my door, you were very angry. I wouldn't dare hit you, I want to help you, so I cast out the spirit of anger. I said, you're not angry anymore right. She nodded in agreement.

I was told later that Ms. C had a problem with anger for a long time. She had run-ins with several other teachers. After the spirit of anger was cast out she became pleasant and soft spoken. I was at that school all year long. She was a pleasure to work with after that day. One teacher told me she didn't know Ms. C could be so nice. When evil is cast out, and Jesus comes in, things are always better.

WHERE IS MY SISTER?

I moved into a new neighborhood. I went door to door witnessing. The first house I came to was an older lady who was refined to bed. I introduced myself to her and asked if there was anything I could do to help her. She told me she was sick and had been sick for a while. I asked if I could fix her some food. She nodded yes. I warmed some soup for her and hand-fed it to her. I told her how special she was to the Lord and how much He loved her. I asked if she wanted me to pray for her before I left. She said yes. When I laid hands on her to pray for her, the enemy said when she is not healed you are going to shame God. This woman is really sick. I prayed Lord guide me. The Lord spoke to me and said, all I asked you to do is pray, I never asked you to heal anyone. I prayed the prayer of healing and deliverance.

That evening a woman knocked at my door. Have you seen my sister, she asked. She explained where she lived. I told her I had seen her sister earlier. I volunteered to help her find her sister. She went south I went north on our street. I didn't find her, but I met she and her sister when I was returning. What happened I asked. After you left the Lord touched and healed my body; I felt so good; I just wanted to go and visit my friend; I left the house walking; I walked all the way to my friend's house, the lady explained. Isn't the Lord Great!

CARE FOR ME

The Lord led me to visit a neighboring church. At the church I saw an older woman who was sickly. The Lord spoke to me and said care for her. I introduced myself to the lady and her daughter and offered to come by to help her. The daughter gladly agreed.

Monday I arrived at their home. I told the daughter I felt the Lord wanted me to help her mother and help her with her mother. The daughter was overjoyed, she was caring for her mother and her baby. I knew it was hard for her. I took over complete care of her mother. I cooked for her, I washed her up, and I read the Bible to her. We also sang together and prayed together. If the daughter was out or away I stayed with the mother. I became a second daughter to her. Everything I did was unto the Lord. The Lord had told me to care for her. He had given me the mind to do it.

I cared for her many months. I tried to preach faith to her, but she believed God only healed some people. Her condition worsen. She had Parkinson's disease. She shook so badly she could not hold things in her hands without dropping them.

We had to take her to the hospital. I stayed with her while she was there. In her hospital room, we were watching a well known preacher on TV. He was preaching about the rapture of the church, and how the dead in Christ would rise first. I knew the Lord was going to take her home soon. I said, this message is just for you. She had a far-away stare in her eyes.

When the program was over dinner was served. I gave thanks and said a Bible verse before feeding her. I said Psalms 23:1 "The Lord is my Shepherd, I shall not want." She said, hump, I'm always wanting. I said no, we don't say that, and we don't feel that way. The Lord loves you and we love the Lord. He is our Shepherd. He did not make you sick. She agreed, saying she was just tired. She ate a little food, before pushing it away.

I saw her staring out the window again. What do you see I asked. She didn't answer. I walked around to the left side of her bed to straighten her covers. When I turned to sit, she grabbed my arm and said, I'm afraid. I knew what she meant. I looked her in the eye and said, this is not how saints die. We are not afraid to die because we know the truth. I'm afraid to die, she said. I said, God loves you. When it's time for you to die He will send an angel for you. You are special to Him. Let's pray, I said, and rebuke this evil spirit of fear. Fear is not from the Lord. We prayed. when we ended our prayer she let go of my arm. She said it's all right now. She went to be with the Lord the next day.

TAKE ME LORD

A sixty year old nurse in our church was diagnosed with cancer. She was from New York state. She had two boys. One in high school and one grown. She deteriorated rapidly. Her sister from New York came to bring her home. She didn't have a husband. Her boys waited till high school was out since they only had a short time left.

The boys needed someone to drive them to New York which was a thirteen hour trip. I felt the Lord wanted me to drive them. He had given me a message for their mother.

On the way there the grow-up son became very abusive verbally. He gave me the impression he might even become physically abusive. We were in New York state, but still about three hours from their place. I repeatedly warned the young man, but he ignored me. I saw a police car along the highway. I pulled up behind it. I explained my situation to the policeman and asked for his advice. He talked to the young man who got smart with him. He suggested I leave the young man with him and he'd put him on a bus home. I asked the young man if he would be willing to sit quiet the rest of the trip if he rode in the car, he refused. I left him with the policeman who took him to the bus station.

When we got to New York their mother was very weak. She was skin and bones. I didn't recognize her at first. After I rested a little, we talked and prayed together. Her sixteen year old had told her how badly her older son had acted and she felt bad. I tried to tell her it was all right. We began to talk. She told me she was ready to go, but there was something she needed to do. She wasn't sure what that was. Let's pray and ask the Lord what it is, I said. We prayed. After prayer I knew what it was she needed to do.

The Lord said you need to forgive sister. I don't know what, but I'm sure the Lord will show you. She began to cry and say, you're right that's it, I didn't know I hadn't forgiven, but when you said that I needed to forgive, I vividly saw two situations that happened years ago. I pushed them out of my mind, but I didn't forgive them. I want to pray and forgive them now. We prayed. As she prayed and released everything she began to praise the Lord. Her face glowed with the light of the Lord. She said she felt like great weights had been lifted from her. She went to be with the Lord the next week. Praise God!

AUTHORITY IN JESUS NAME

When God first placed man in the garden of Eden, He gave man dominion over everything. Man however, lost this dominion or Lordship when he sinned. But when Jesus became a living sacrafice for sin, He paid the price for us and restored us to our original place of Lordship. We once again have dominion over all creatures in the name of Jesus. I had an opportunity to use this authority while in Japan.

When I moved into my apartment, my Japanese friend Masumi was helping me move. She told me I would probably have roaches in the apartment because roaches were everywhere in Japan. I told her I would not have roaches in my apartment. I have not lived with them before and I won't live with them now, I said.

Masumi took me by the hand and walked me over to where the water meter was. She opened the lid on the ground, and I saw what looked like milllions of roaches covering the underground lid. I remembered who I was and I spoke to the roaches in jesus name and I said to them, "roaches , you will not come into my house in Jesus name. If you come into my house you will die immediately in the name of Jesus." Masumi looked at me as if I was crazy. Do you really believe that, she asked. I believe every word of it I said. Jesus has given us dominion over every creature, and I will not have roaches in my house.

She closed the lid and we started walking toward the apartment. As we walked, I looked down and there was a roach walking with us. I spoke to the roach and I said, You will not go into my house, if you attempt to go into my house you will die. As we continued to walk, Masumi commented that the roach was still walking with us.

When we got to the door of my apartment I looked down and sure enough the roach had continued to follow us. As we walked inside of the apartment Masumi and I both looked at the roach to see what it would do. The roach approached the threshold of the door's entrance, and it was as if it could not go foward, the roach died there I and discarded it. From that day to the day I left Japan I never had roaches in my apartment. Because of the shed blood of Jesus and the power of His resurrection from the dead, we have dominion over every creature in His name. Jesus is Lord of Lords and He is the King of Kings Amen.

A SPEAKER

While in New York I stayed at the house of one of the church members. She was a sweet sister with three children and a loving husband. She had prayer at her home on Tuesday nights. I met with the prayer group that Tuesday. The leader of the group asked us to agree in prayer with her about a speaker for a women's convention they had scheduled for the following week. She explained how the Lord was saying no to everyone she suggested. This was the first time, she said, they didn't have a speaker scheduled. We prayed and agreed with her. I had to leave early. As I was leaving the leader stopped me, and said the Lord said, you are our speaker. Are you sure the Lord said me, I'm so tired from traveling. Please pray about it tonight, and let me know tomorrow, she said.

When I prayed the Lord said He would give me what to say. I shared this information with the leader. She was overjoyed. The meeting was set. She said they had rented a building downtown that held at least two thousand. The day of the meeting, the place was packed. When I ministered the Word I felt the Holy Ghost anointing on me more strongly than I ever had before. When the people came forth for prayer, before they had a chance to say what it was they needed prayer for the Holy Ghost revealed it to me and I prayed for them. Only the Lord could have told you, many said. The Lord gave a great deliverance. Many were healed, delivered and set free. I had never been in a service where the Holy Ghost was in control like that. It was more beautiful than words can say.

The Lord is so awesome. I wish I knew words to describe

his greatness. I could go on and never stop telling of the good things He's done for me and others. He is a good God. There is no limit to what He can do and there is no limit to what He will do for us. Jesus is alive and He still works miracles. Praise be the name of the Lord and the precious Son of God, JESUS! I LOVE YOU LORD.

Manufactured By: RR Donnelley
Momence, IL USA
June, 2010